Grieve

Stories and Poems
about Grief and Loss

Volume 2

HUNTER WRITERS CENTRE

Grieve Volume 2
Hunter Writers Centre
Newcastle NSW 2300

Email: publishing@hunterwriterscentre.org
Website: www.grieveproject.org

Grieve: Stories and Poems about Grief and Loss

22 21 20 19 18   1 2 3 4 5
ISBN-978-0-9954409-8-2 (paperback)

Cover design by HWC Publishing
Typesetting by HWC Publishing
2014 Published by Hunter Writers Centre Inc.

© Each short story/poem is copyright of the respective author
© This collection copyright of Hunter Writers Centre

All rights reserved.
No part of this publication may be reproduced, stored in a retrieval system, or transmitted in any form by any means electronic, mechanical, photocopying, recording or otherwise without the prior consent of the publishers.

Table of Contents

In Her Day — 1
Sharon Elisara

A Letter From The Land Of Alone — 2
Megan Buxton

Ancient Grief — 4
Linda Brooks

The Letter — 6
Ted Bassingthwaighte

The Waiting Room — 8
Tara Ali

Your Granddaughter Asks What You Think of Tattoos — 10
Kristin Henry

Crossroads — 11
Janet Upcher

Desolation — 12
Ashton von Westmeath

For a Moment — 14
S.E. Street

Chasing Butterflies — 15
Anna Minska

The Tree — 16
Janet Lee

Strings of Light Upon Us — 18
Alison Martin

An Explanation — 20
Rebecca Edwards

In Came the Doctor — 22
Nikki Moyes

The Stroking — 24
Kevin Gillam

Blue Balloon — 26
Penny Lane

Fractured Grief — 28
Tiffany Neill

Making Peace with the Impossible Beast — 29
Liana Joy Christensen

Kaleidoscope — 30
Jessica Mienert

Bearing Witness — 32
Elsa Kurt

The White Sheet — 34
Lesley Beards

Mary Margaret — 36
Marie McMillan

Braver, Stronger, Kinder — 38
Gillian Swain

Harlequin — 39
Anthony Wood

The Maxi Taxi — 40
Janey Runci

The Earth Turned Over — 42
Phillip Radmall

Grey Matter — 43
Rebecca Niumeitolu

Inertia — 44
Rhonda Wilson

Grieving for my mother — 45
Jena Woodhouse

My Mother Died — 46
Lorraine Chapman

Grieving the Double Helix — 47
Magdalena Ball

Grieving Hamish — 48
Rachel Noble

Babe of Me — 49
Margaret Polacska

Votive Jane Symonds	50
The Northerly Andrea Lagana	51
Dog Bite M.J. Reidy	52
Loss of Intimacy Desney King	54
Memories of the Mountains Elizabeth Sutherland	56
Are You There? Karen McRae	57
A Consequence of War Burt Candy	58
The Shape of Life Holly Bruce	60
Diptych: Grief Wakes Mark Miller	61
Time and Place Stolen Jennifer Lavoipierre	62
Six Wednesdays Dionne Mence	64
He Opted for Heaven Kate-Lyn Therkelsen	66
Thylacine Lisa Jacobson	67
Solstice Suzi Mezei	68
A Constant Absence Amanda Berry	70
Schism Suzi Mezei	72
June's Death Hazel Barker	74

Party — 76
Heather Taylor Johnson

Husband — 77
Diane Barkas

Like Father, Like Son — 78
Fiona Macdonald

Why — 80
Tania Connolly

The Woman Who Wasn't To Be — 81
Jackie Macdonald

I Grieve — 82
John Hall

Tom — 84
Simone Mackinnon

The Art of Grief — 86
Bindy Pritchard

Coming and Going — 88
Karina Quinn

Don't Shut the Door — 90
Mireille Bucher

Warmth — 91
Lisa Fritz

Vanished — 92
Kate Robin-White

Whitewash — 94
Bronwyn Lovell

I Think — 95
Sarah Whitaker

The Bingo Game — 96
Johanna Emily Gilman

Michael — 98
Ann Blackwell

Everflow — 100
Kimberley Hodge-Freed

My Journey   101
Sue Masens

Dear Sister   102
Mary Alys Shuttleworth

Diploma of Grief   104
Nicki Reed

Wisdom has Come   106
Roger Vickery

After the News   107
Kathryn Fry

Orange   108
Nicole Gill

Water   110
Hanna Schenkel

Mum's Place   112
Kynan Cliff

Grief   113
Lydia C. Lee

I've learned that people will forget what you said, people will forget what you did, but people will never forget how you made them feel.

- Maya Angelou

Introduction

It can be enriching, uplifting—perhaps cathartic—to make the decision to write about grief: to put pen to paper in order to express the complex, overwhelming, and sometimes dark feelings that loss can bring.

The stories, personal essays and poems in this anthology capture the confusion, anger, stoicism, forgiveness, acceptance and hope that we humans often feel in the face of loss and grief.

When we consider how many pieces here show us unrecognised, ignored and avoided grief we know there are many more volumes of Grieve that can be published. This volume is only one of many already published and of many to come.

Literature, like all art forms, offers the opportunity for us to put order and form to our feelings, to take our jumbled thoughts and lay them out in a way that is true to us, an expression of our experience or what we witness of the experience for others.

Writing offers the chance to be direct and honest through the telling of the details and specifics of our experience. Yet, despite the specificity, time and time again, we find the works reach us because of their universality.

This is the magic of good writing—the details revealing the universal—shown here and in all the volumes of Grieve.

Karen Crofts
Director
Hunter Writers Centre
Australia
www.grieveproject.org

In Her Day

Sharon Elisara

Ivy has never told anyone, but she used to see her. Not all the time. Just every now and then. All of a sudden there she was. At the park, on the bus, at the shops. Blonde and blue-eyed, always laughing, just as she imagined. Sometimes she had even followed her for a while, just to see what she would have been like. But then she looked for her in every little girl, always hoping for a glimpse of the child she had never known.

Ivy was never allowed to see her, let alone hold her, that's how it was in her day. The tiny lifeless body wrapped up and whisked away before she had even realised that her baby was dead. They never even told her where they'd taken her. She likes to think she is buried in a shared coffin, then she wouldn't be alone. It worries Ivy to think she is alone.

She looks down at her wrinkled time worn hands. Nowadays she is so forgetful, yet, she's never been able to forget the very thing she was supposed to. Bill had been in the waiting room and, when they finally let him see her, they had cried together. But he hadn't known what to say. They told you to forget and that is what he'd done, never speaking of it again. Nearly fifty years later as he lay dying she had almost said 'I called her Elizabeth' but that wouldn't have been fair.

Ivy had done the right thing at the time, producing two strapping boys in quick succession. She hadn't minded just having boys. In some ways it made moving on a little easier, but it always hurt when well meaning people would say it was a shame she had never had a daughter.

She pulls her hanky out from under her cuff. She always keeps one there. She seems to need it so often nowadays. She feels so silly, a woman of her age crying all the time, especially about something that happened so long ago.

She thinks about how different things are these days. You are encouraged to grieve. She would be able to hold her little girl for as long as she needed, and she would have photos, or maybe even casts of her little hands and feet. There would be a proper funeral, and a grave to visit.

Ivy doesn't try to stop the tears she has been ignoring for fifty years. Since Bill's been gone she can't help thinking about what will happen when she goes. If she doesn't tell someone it will be as if Elizabeth never existed. She has lived her whole life without her daughter, she won't die without her as well. She takes a deep breath as the tears flow. Tomorrow she will call the boys.

She has never cried in front of her children. You just didn't do that in her day – but then her days are nearly over.

A Letter From The Land Of Alone

Megan Buxton

Dear You,

I'm standing in your room. If I breathe deep enough I can smell the cinnamon scent of you. If I'm still enough I can feel a tiny tremor of your essence. If I'm quiet I can hear you, but you're as faint as the echo of bird call in a canyon. And you're fading.

I put your things away today in cardboard boxes. Six of them. How can they, so flimsy in substance and so small in number, hold all the love and the dreams and the hope that I've packed away inside them.

There they squat, like toadstools on the bedroom floor. And I don't know what to do with them now they're full. How can I give away the things you touched, the clothes that once touched you? I'm scared that, if I let them go, there'll be nothing left to remind me of you.

Death took you and as he left, he poked holes in me so the heart of me leaked out. I zombie-shuffle through my days dressed in black. You hated black, but colours are for the living; they hurt my grieving eyes.

It's funny – in a sad, strange way. You died and I'm like a corpse.

And here I am in the land of alone. And it's hard here.

People talk about my 'late' daughter. How I wish that were true and any moment you would burst through the door, scattering your belongings like confetti. How I wish that death was just a lack of punctuality.

'Try to think about the good times,' they tell me.

I wonder how that's supposed to help.

Thinking of the good times is vinegar on raw flesh and opens up the wound to bleed memories of arguments and petty jealousies, pointless anger, bitterness. All thrown so carelessly back then when I thought I had forever. Never retracted, never recanted. Lost chances and disappointments.

I feel the awful loneliness of regret.

'Give it time,' they say.

But grief is a ravenous beast. I've been feeding him time and all he wants is more. More time, more pain, more of me. He takes and takes and gives nothing in return.

I've said those same words to others in the past. They sound the same here in the land of alone but their meanings shimmer like mirages and I don't seem to have a dictionary.

And the words don't tell me what to call myself. I'm not an orphan; I still have parents. I'm not a widow; it's not a husband I've lost. No-one has a word for the mother who's lost a child. So what have I become? What am I without you?

'This will pass,' they tell me. I know they're wrong.

Anger ends. Happiness and laughter end. Why, then, does grief go on and on?

Ancient Grief
Linda Brooks

Her eyes are shiny-bright with unshed tears. Like hardened diamonds, unseeing but not unknowing. What she now knows she cannot share; cannot face. She sits amidst the others in the low care ward, in the place for which she has no name. She is 89, and for all those around her she is essentially alone; surrounded by people but isolated by grief. Whether bending over the dining table or clutching her walking stick with grim determination she still manages to appear erect, although she has not been straight-of-back for many years.

Her son died a week ago. He was 71 – in the eyes of many, an old man, but not to her, she who is older than him by the years of her motherhood. She measures all the years and days by her sons, now two. She rose early the day after he died, putting two curlers in her hair as she usually did. Then took them out again before going to the dining room for breakfast. As she always did.

She puts her make-up on as usual but, now, with trembling hand, heavier and imprecise. She walks a little slower; stays a little longer at the table. She brushes the crumbs from her skirt with an absent gaze that glances but never connects with her fellow residents. These little signs are the only indication of her breaking heart.

We do not know how to go to her, in this world of her devastation. She is from a generation where emotions have 'their place'. She will not allow us entrance to her grief, so we must leave her there, in the memorial of her own choosing.

Reaching out with guarded hand she gently touches her son's face, in the photograph by her bedside, when she thinks we're not watching. The tears struggle down her wrinkled cheeks. She hears a door open. She is so afraid to be seen exposed and vulnerable that she flees to the bathroom, to the shower, and the comfort of solitary grieving.

These are the routines she clings to desperately every day for two weeks. But like an autumn leaf she falls. Unable to fall into her grief, she falls in the shower. We find her naked and bleeding, broken and alone. The ambulance comes and she is stoic still.

When she returns from the hospital she is a little more stooped, a little more fragile. Then she begins to sit in the foyer where she has never sat before. When we ask her why, she focuses us with clear, direct eyes. 'I am waiting for the school bus.'

Leaving our reality, she has found her own. She has wandered to a safe place; a place still inhabited by everyone precious to her. Grieving and memories have combined in this new world. She lets us lead her. She doesn't ask to return to her room as once was her custom.

'Take me home,' she whispers.

The Letter

Ted Bassingthwaighte

The Officer in charge
Temora Police Station

Dear Sir,
   I write to you about the conduct of Constable Johnson in your Command. Driving to Temora from Canberra the reality of losing my brother in such sad circumstances, coupled with the swelling realisation of the horrible mess he left was almost unbearable. My anxiety vanished the moment I met Constable Johnson.
   I close my eyes and try to imagine the scene your officer confronted. The smell and horror is beyond my comprehension. He did something for me, my family and, most importantly, my brother that no-one could ever have expected.
   Constable Johnson removed all the perishable goods and unwanted waste of my brother's life. He disinfected and aired the van, restoring the interior to a state that shielded me from additional torment. Nothing was too much trouble for him.
   His actions, in circumstances that must have been distressing for him, deserve my deep thanks and that of my family.
   I ask that you officially thank him.

Yours faithfully,
Ross Allan

My home is a small, white 1983 Nissan tray top with a camper module on the back. I have been driving east from the minefields of Western Australia for about a week or so. The isolation I coveted in that place proved too cruel a master.
   I drink every day to get drunk. It's been like that ever since I was a teenager. They sacked me in Kalgoorlie for being drunk at work.
   I'm not sure why I headed back east. I had nowhere else to go I suppose. Sometimes the pull of the ocean decides where I go. I miss the east coast but not the childhood memories it harbours.
   My older brother Ross lives in Canberra with his family. We haven't spoken for years.
   It is a couple of days before Christmas. I pull off the Newell Highway into a gangers' clearing next to the railway line about ten kilometres out of Temora, NSW. No one can see me parked here. I finish off the flagon

of port I bought in Griffith that morning.

By Boxing Day it's 40 degrees and windless. A uniformed police officer from Temora arrives at the clearing. He approaches carefully. A train driver reported seeing my van parked here for the past week.

The passenger cabin is locked. No keys in the ignition. On the front seat among the jumble of my life he sees a short handwritten note scrawled on a crumpled Centrelink letter.

Walking to rear of the camper he doesn't notice the black hose attached to the exhaust and poking up through a hole in the floor. He forces the door. I am deeply sorry for the scene that confronts him. It doesn't smell good. I never wanted to harm anyone.

The coroner's report was unremarkable: carbon monoxide poisoning – suicide note present – no suspicious circumstances.

The Waiting Room
Tara Ali

The nurse calls out, 'Number 12.'

The pathology waiting room is humming. Bodies hunched over on hard plastic seats, eyes fixated on Candy Crush, Facebook. The low-level chatter of morning TV presenters. Anxious limbs, jittering on plastic seats. Phones ringing. Receptionist papers shuffling. Styrofoam caffeine and sterile air. Number 12 is an overweight man in a parka jacket. His wife looks on as he gets up, face crumpled with concern. She zips a pendant on her gold necklace left and right. By the time my turn comes I've heard many hushed words from numbers 13 to 17: painful bladders. Heavy pregnancy. Worrying chest pains. 'Number 18.'

My nurse is strikingly tall. Slim frame. Early fifties. I don't notice much else. Plastic gloves snapping, kidney-shaped tray placed on the counter, four carefully selected test tubes dropped inside. She props my arm on a pillow and I let her know I need a butterfly needle for my tiny veins. Mouth pursed. I explain that I'm doing IVF, needles are a big part of my life right now.

She wipes the alcohol swab on my elbow crook. I squeeze a fist. Sting, in goes the tip. I stare at the wall.

'Oh yes, I know,' she says. 'I went through the IVF process myself years ago. No heavy lifting, bruises are sometimes common, drink plenty of water.'

I hesitate to ask if she was successful. I need stories of hope right now. I've been searching for signs everywhere. Counting magpies: One for sorrow, two for joy, three for a girl, four for a boy. Silence. My voice box goes ahead. And then suddenly I notice everything about her.

Her answer is whispered and yet one thousand decibels.

'Yes. Well, no.'

I want her to stop, but it's too late. She withdraws the needle and speaks. Her words are stoic. Strung tight. Bathed in numbness. Bound by factuality. Presses on the puncture wound with cotton wool. She carried two babies to 20 weeks and another was born at 26 weeks. Unwraps a Band Aid.

'You never get over it.'

Her blonde hair. Her lack of wedding ring. Fragility. Our eyes connect and I see in this woman the many years of her. I witness just a tiny fragment of her pain. There in that room works another mother-in-waiting. She sees it in me and I in her and my heart breaks for her lost dreams.

There is nothing to be said but, 'Oh I'm so sorry.' Never have my words felt so trite. We both breathe in, I pick up my jacket, tell her she is a good blood taker and she grabs on to the subject change with a leap. But we both know. I have seen her grief and she has felt my hope.

And so vivid is this woman's life that I get in my car and I cry, for all the mothers left in the waiting room. Please let me step out one day.

Your Granddaughter Asks What You Think of Tattoos
Kristin Henry

Careful, you tell yourself. Careful.
This may be some teenage test you can't afford to fail.
She's seventeen, and full of surprises.
Her mother – your daughter – is four years gone.
And mostly the two of you bear this injustice
quietly, as though somehow grief is your guilt.

Careful, you tell yourself. Do not judge,
on no account sound old.
Aim for neutral, fall back on the law;
tell her she must wait at least a year.
I know, she says, and smiles. But do you want to see?

And for just a breath you hesitate
on another question you're not sure how to answer.
Life has shown you too many wrongs
which can never be corrected.
Do you really need to see another one?

But your eyes widen on a miracle
when the girl lifts her shirt to show
the small blue message curling across
the ribs beneath her heart. You recognise the writing,
know the slope and shape of every letter
because it is your daughter's.

Among her mother's things the child has found a journal,
and copied precisely a line, then had it etched
into her flesh, and her memory and her future.
In her mother's hand, her mother's words –
this delicate, elastic, indelible truth –
I will love you always.

Crossroads
Janet Upcher

You are the son
grown to manhood,
You were the tiny bird
fluttering in the womb,
you were the small mammal
nibbling at the nipple,
the schoolboy who defied gravity
on a skateboard,
the student who glittered and flew high
and still you are flying.

Fly away, scholar,
a new universe, new university,
new hemisphere awaits;
you are crossing a threshold,
no turning back.
Your room is a hollow nest;
'If I don't come back, Mum,
 you can sell what's left …'

And now, that hour at the airport,
time's arrow takes aim at the heart.
You lean to me in a last embrace
choking a sob that crests in your throat
I feel the heave in your chest
the cleave in my own
I think of all children leaving,
all mothers left in war and in peace.
'Boarding pass… you're together?'
'No. I'm alone.'
Metal doors slide open
my heart clangs shut.
last clasp of the hand, the final cut
as you disappear behind steel.
Your after-shave lingers for weeks
like the after-blindness of love,
the after-numbness of grief.

Desolation
Ashton von Westmeath

They were gentle and kind. One, quite unselfconsciously, held my hand as if junior policemen always held the hands of numbed fathers. Perhaps they do. I kept thinking of preparing her horse for shows, the burnishing of tack, of cold dawn starts; the misty echo of our words hanging in the air.

She was wearing a burgundy silk dress, the colour highlighting the pallor of her skin and the heavy waves of raven hair. Her closed eyes and long lashes reminding me of childhood nights watching her sleep.

You think that you should cry, but inside there is a desert of pain that swallows tears. Instead your mind, seeking meaning, tries to apportionblame. Then there is guilt. 'If I had done this or that, then this black hole of emptiness would not be eating tomorrow for ever and ever and ever.'

The room service waiter said that when she called for coffee, a little after midnight, he found her by the window looking at the lights reflected in the harbour. He commented on the beauty of the view and remembered her reply. 'Yes, it makes you glad to be alive.' It must have been just after that that she started taking the pills, washing them down with coffee and looking at the view. In the morning there was some coffee left and she was sitting by the window.

Listen, there is nothing worse than this; nothing. Friends seeking to comfort, prattle on about time being a great healer and in some sense they are right. The edge goes from the pain, then a smell, a piece of music, a turned head in a crowd rips the callus of time away and the wound is as fresh as today's bread.

Newborn, I held her and knew that I walked with gods. Through dependent childhood, rebellious adolescence and the confidence of maturity this sense of wonder and all enveloping love formed a base note underlying the music of life. We knew, of course, that the various treatments had failed but unfounded hope is always there buttressed by the feeling that we somehow have immunity from disaster. We could only guess at the pain, in the end, so overwhelming.

I kept thinking that she should have told of her intention, that we would have understood, not tried to prevent it, but she knew us better than we knew ourselves. I know that I would have had a thousand reasons for delay, 'just for today' and then for 'just another day', with life measured in increments of pain and helplessness. As her letter said, 'You're a soft old bastard, so my way is best.'

Her horse grazes the home paddock and in winter when frost cracks underfoot, the magpies call and my breath still hangs in the air. I can see her in my mind's eye, mounted, back straight, heels down, hands gentle, and I rejoice in her life, and count the pain as cheap for the joy that was mine.

For a Moment
S.E. Street

I had already seen many distant deaths,
the inexplicable: tiny babies and small children
and the inevitable: the aged and world weary
but this boy, dying of a brain tumour
at eighteen, was a year younger than me.

From the nurses' desk, I had watched his mother gather herself outside his door,
breathing deeply,
rolling her shoulders back,
fabricating a smile
before she entered to hold her handsome, long-limbed son,
less than a year ago: Captain of Rowing, Captain of Rugby.

It was the end of my shift; I was heading for the stairs,
for Saturday night, car keys in my hand
but as I passed his door she leant out and asked if I could stay with him
for a moment
while she moved her car.

He was asleep, so I stood by the window,
a grey, bare-treed, winter afternoon.
The sounds of a rugby game on the hospital oval,
a cheering crowd,
the long final whistle
assailed the room.
The world was playing on
and I turned to see if the barbs of noise had found their mark.

He was awake, watching me.
Rallying a deep breath, he whispered *'Come here.'*
I perched on the side of the bed.
'Let down your hair.'
At that moment, my thoughts were of a passing matron
but I let my hair fall in a curtain across his chest.
He slipped his fingers up and held them there,
drifting back to sleep.

I heard the door open and close behind me.
His mother quietly crying.

Chasing Butterflies
Anna Minska

i loved you in the endless corridors
       of your mind. we chased fractured
       thoughts like butterflies through a carpet
       of nasturtiums needing to believe
       we were under
       blue sky.

i loved you swaddled in pages
       of the Freudian fairytale keeping you
       safe at night and rolling me into dreams
       of who you might have been if babbling inkblots with damning
       wings ever stayed still long enough to be translated
       into the mother tongue.

i loved you when you had me pinned
       upside-down against the corner
       of the hard facts they dug up. you swore
       fallacy on desperate knee reeling
       in and stitching up your prized freedom
       collectible. That room you framed me in had a million-dollar view
       of the contested ground in need of leveling.

i loved you when the broth bubbled
       over and ultimatums cracked under the pressure
       of truthful impulse. I released into air and left you
       trapped in the seething kitchen
       muttering prophecies into the sink.

i love you still from this devastating distance
       that regulates my hopeful instincts. daily
       i dance with the echoes of your cacophonic opus
       and draw myself downwards
       exiled ether breathing new lines onto mangled maps
       of the world you scored for me.

The Tree
Janet Lee

The tree which marks your death is dying.

It is taking its time, drawn into a slow, withering death. It weakens and fades in a way you never did.

I planted it that week. That week 37 years and 5 months ago when you ceased to be. When you were sucked from my body, a tiny blood clot not permitted to be more. Pulled from me with steel spoons by those who spend their days scooping unviable souls from the wombs of women.

I could not mourn you. So, I planted you a tree, that you might have a place on this earth. That you might live and breathe and feel the sun.

I chose a pine that would live for a thousand years. And yet, before its time, it dies. Just as you did.

They build test-tube babies now. No lust required, just mix sperm and egg together as a cocktail, pardon the pun. A better way to create children, freeze them and use them later, part of the instant gratification society. I expect we will buy test tube babies in the freezer section of the supermarket soon.

If I could have frozen you, I would have. I would have waited to grow you later, when I had the time or money or whatever it was that I needed to let me keep you. I would have. I would have.

But I couldn't.

The babies in the test tubes they don't get sucked out, they get thawed. Their owners pay to have them snap frozen and when babies are no longer wanted they are thawed. Taken out of the freezer to slowly die on a bench top. I have a friend who thawed 42. She talked openly of 42 tiny souls taken from their glass tubes and left to die. She did not mourn. She did not plant 42 trees.

I have no right to sadness because I killed you. It was my decision, my choice, and my loss.

I cannot share my pain. They would scorn me as a fallen woman. As an evil killer. As I am.

Only my mother, who arranged your death, only she knew of my pain. She is long dead herself now. Perhaps you have met her? That would have been awkward I imagine.

I imagine lots of things.

I have no other children and am looked on as a barren, sexless female. And yet I have had you, my child, grown tall and lush like your tree. I cannot imagine why you die when you have so much before you. I chose a pine that you may live for a thousand years, yet you lived only 37.

As you wither and die, I can fall to my knees and sob. Strangers may pass and wonder at the madness of this woman who lays prone at a tree.

But they do not know how I mourn.

Your tree dies, and I am fallen into despair.

I grieve.

Strings of Light Upon Us
Alison Martin

We know they are watching
Our disbanded bones
      Straying into the orphaned day.

The Sun, stifled and bound in the cupola sky,
Meandering distress
      Twirling between our untouching fingertips.

I know they are watching
When the words form and fail upon my swelling, indistinct tongue.
It is like trying to sing through a mouthful of marbles,
Like trying to kiss with blood-lumbered lips.

And what of this, this fragmented collarbone
Melting into barren breast?
And what of these, these shadowless feet,
Dislocated from their silhouettes?

You and me, our muffled footfalls
Dissolving into awkward puddles:
We visit unease into the bone-framed firm bodies of the rest.

They see us in our provocative sorrow:
The way the sun skips our brows
And settles somewhere else.

Where are the cartographers to map this sterile chasm?
Where are those with instruments to chart these starless skies?
It is like trying to see through an underwater forest,
Like trying to prise apart the jaws of an undying night.

We will weep, again, again, tomorrow
When another unborn morning engenders an empty shadow.
When the bones of a boy, forever formless,
Are yet, still, eternally unborne.

But if only you could hold my wrist
Between your thumb and middle finger - a loose encircling -
Together we could anchor our bones to the earth.
Together we could watch the Sun
Unsmother, unbind from the cupola sky,
Begin to unfurl
Strings of light upon us.

An Explanation
Rebecca Edwards

You were too shy. You were reluctant to face the jagged branches, the sharp-winged birds.

'A little mouse,' your father said as we stood before the screen. It held six photographs of you. Six stills.

'I'll give you some time,' said the radiologist. 'You don't have to leave through the front. I'll let reception know.'

Her name is Julie, she tells us, as she ushers us into the consulting room. I lie down on the bed and lift my shirt. I am still hoping for good news.

Paul sits where he can see the screen. I watch the radiologist. Her face tightens as she draws the transducer across my belly.

'Do you want me to tell you what I'm seeing?'

'Yes.'

'Are you sure?'

I reach out for Paul's hand. The radiologist turns the screen towards me.

'Here is the foetus.' She points to a grey blob at the bottom of a grainy black cone. 'I should be able to see a heart-beat, a little flash, just here.'

I squeeze Paul's hand, still hoping, because she has not yet said.

'I am going to keep looking because I would hate to be wrong.' She clicks a button on the transducer's side. Patches of red and orange appear amongst the grey.

'I'm checking for blood flow.'

There are no red or orange patches on your body. I start to cry.

'I'm sorry,' I say to Paul. 'I'm so sorry.'

'It's not your fault,' he says.

'I'm still looking for a heart-beat,' says the radiologist. I hold my breath. We watch the ridgeline of your chest.

You do not move.

'Poor little thing.' I'm crying again.

'It doesn't know,' says the radiologist immediately. 'You are the one who is suffering.'

Then she says: 'It was nine weeks and five days old.'

Soon I am allowed to get up.

'Take your time.' She closes the door gently behind her.

We go back through reception because we don't know how else to leave. The receptionists don't stop us or ask us to pay nor do they ask us if we would like a picture to take home.

Paul has to go back to work. A deadline is due. In engineering terms it is called a 'deliverable'.

I get out at the lights across from the church. I could go there and talk to someone. Paul's car swings around the corner, heading down the hill, and I wave.

I don't cross at the lights. I don't go to the church. I don't have anything to say.

On the walk home I smell eucalyptus and honey. Sulphur-crested cockatoos tear at flowers above my head. A thin autumn sun shines against my back. The thought comes to me that you were too shy.

You died without knowing you were alive.

'A little mouse,' your father said and touched you on the screen.

Now we have to let you go.

In Came the Doctor
Nikki Moyes

I sink into a squishy orange chair, hold my hands in my lap and glance out the observation window to the secure nurses' station where they took my bag after I emptied my pockets. The doctor, nurse and psychiatrist crowd the small room discussing my arrival while the psychiatrist's student clutches his note pad and stares at the tired grey carpet.

The scene reminds me of a rhyme from my childhood.
In came the Doctor,
In came the Nurse,
In came the lady with the alligator purse.

My mind jumps to strange thoughts at inappropriate times. Does this happen to other people? Maybe it's not such a surprise to find myself in the secure ward of the mental hospital.

The doctor checks his watch and the men file out the door, closing it behind them, for my own protection. I'm locked in here. Alone with my thoughts. I dig my finger nails into my palms and focus on calming my breathing.

Sometime later, the doctor opens my door and ushers in a patient who moves with the slow, disorientated movements of an old man. His unruly, ginger curls clash with the tight pink t-shirt. It takes a moment before I can convince myself it's him.

His name is Toby, age thirty-four. We met when I was eighteen. He hates anything tight around his neck which is why he always wears collared shirts. He hesitates when he sees me, confused by the change in routine. There's no recognition on his face.

'Dead,' said the Doctor,
'Dead,' said the Nurse,
'Dead,' said the lady with the alligator purse.

He shuffles in and sits two chairs away from me. His entourage follows, crowding the room, waiting to see how he reacts.

'Do you know who I am?' I ask.

He shakes his head. He always got annoyed with me if I did that. Speak, he would say. The backs of my eyes sting as the medical staff, satisfied he will sit quietly, file out of the room.

Out went the Doctor.

How do you hold a conversation with someone whose memory spans only a few hours? There is nothing before that for him. I sit alone for half an hour as he slowly drowns in a sea of tears and snot, stemmed by a single soggy tissue.

I have to go back to work. One of us has to remain a functioning adult. The door has been left ajar this time. I leave to find a nurse with a fresh tissue and to let me out of this hell, before I too sink into depression.

'Are you coming back?' the nurse asks. She doesn't wait for an answer.

Out went the Nurse.

As the security door locks behind me, I can't help but think suicide would have been easier to grieve than this. There is no closure for my loss. I pull myself together and walk out into the sunshine.

Out went the lady with the alligator purse.

The Stroking
Kevin Gillam

(i)

need to walk the boundaries
tonight, walk the fences, keep

the silence in. need to keep
myself jewelled, spangled, bright for

the hour. is grief tidal? need
to follow a new North, fly

to a season of matt-fin-
ished words. a whiff of kelp a-

bout the moon? need to run a
finger across the creped back

of your hand, across purpling.
need to complete the stroking

(ii)

the night hums and in the interval
between breath and moon and soft focus
we unfurl beside the Sound, islands

dolloped on the horizon, from the
rocks, aquamarine and scrub blurring,
gulls apostrophes cut loose, and there's

wide silence here, bar lines through hours un-
played, sea beneath cloud turning tinsel
to truth and this is, was, our stroking

(iii)

drip feeding you sea, in these last hours, quilt of you
barely rippling, music on the edge of silence.
call it unsewing? bloom on the back of your hand,
tenses knocked from you, nurses hovering like bees.
the diameter of solitude? need to shape

a frame, find safe keeping for the shirt box and pins
holding the ward, hour, breathing waning, the stroking.

Blue Balloon
Penny Lane

I lose her every morning.

Wake into grief. Shower. Butter my toast and drizzle it with honey. Eat slowly, savouring the syrupy mouthfuls as I soak in sunlight. Lick my sticky fingers. Read a message on my phone. Fingertip back that I cannot do lunch today. Thx

Rainbow lorikeets shriek from a grevillea, a kookaburra sits alert on the fence.

I move to my desk, switch on my laptop. She smiles at me from the screen and I smile back, my eyes wet. My husband slots James Blunt into the CD player. I open a new document and my hands on the keys choreograph a new story. A character has her eyes, her laugh, but is not her, and does not have her cancer.

I swivel into sunshine and gaze down into the bay and up into the sky. I'm inside a glorious blue balloon.

Remembering a birthday balloon, blue too. A little arm holding it high.

My phone buzzes. I fingertip that I am sorry. Not tomorrow. Thx

I drive to the library. Above the roadside, a pink swoop of galahs. A bluster of eucalyptus leaves. A warm breeze at my ankles when I step from the car. I stand for a few moments to feel the breeze on my skin. In the library, I fill my bag with books to maybe read. Magazines to flip through but maybe not see.

I shop. Buy the season's last peaches, strawberries, prawns. From her photo in my purse she smiles at me. Every shopping day, she smiles her bridal happiness. I buy freshly baked bread, hold the warm loaf and breathe in a waft of sourdough.

'Are you avoiding me?' My texting friend is also buying bread. She walks with me to my car and when I open the boot sees my bag of books, my magazines. 'A bit of escapism,' she says. 'That's what you need.'

I don't wish to escape. I want the life I'm in, its memories held close, the glory of ballooning sea and sky. I open books simply to visit other words and worlds.

Her photo bookmarks pages.

'We must do lunch soon,' my friend says. 'You can't sit at home and hide. You've got to get over it; you've got to move on. It's been three years.'

At home again, prawns piled on fresh bread, lemon slices in iced water. Sitting with my husband outside in the blue balloon. Dolphins scalloping the bay. The leaves of the lemon tree quivering. A slender bronze lizard peeping from a rock crevice, it and I both watchful for a kookaburra.

A stab of memory. A kookaburra and our daughter, nine years old, exchanging laughs as though they were conversing. A watery blink.

The lemon tree reaching its thorny branches to the blue balloon.

'We ought to trim the lemon tree,' I say.

Fractured Grief
Tiffany Neill

Darkness
seeps along a barren room.
Hands barely visible.
Their outline greyed and fading.

A calm surface disguises
a concaved heart
that grief
bruised and drained.

Chills cause shivers,
no blanket can warm.
Trembles ripple
to the bone.

Unforeseen wind blows,
the curtain gently parts.
Light fractures,
sparking against darkness.

Light interrupts,
brightening sombre corners.
Warmth crawls along the veins,
stimulating a beating heart.

Hands illuminated.
Hands visible.

Making Peace with the Impossible Beast

Liana Joy Christensen

For nine days and nine nights live in silence, never looking at the beast, but never moving more than nine steps away.

On the morning of the tenth day it will lay its shaggy head in your lap.

Ignore the smell. Ignore the vermin that seethe in its fur. Stroke it gently and sing lullabies to ease its dying.

Name a star for it and be on your way.

Kaleidoscope

Jessica Mienert

All is monotone at 2am, dust motes colourless as the fabric of my self. Abortion. The word makes me gag. I want to vomit and hiccup and cry all at once.

Waiting is grey. In the ward there are two other women, one sips tea. The television is pointed to them and not me.
'Did you bring something to change into?' quips a mean nurse.
'No.'
A blue cloth is thrust at me 'you can use this as a sarong.' I change in a sterile bathroom with a mushrooming basket of pads on the vanity then wait, sick and alone.
A friendly nurse takes my blood pressure, 'no sex for two weeks.'
'Can you put that in writing please?'
We laugh. My last laugh. I pretend to watch TV while the others discuss football.
Mean nurse approaches, 'this way' across a landing into unchartered territory, 'you're 13 weeks aren't you?'
It's not a crime it's not a crime it's not a crime. I'm due on the sixth of November, a boy I'm sure, headstrong and determined with summer birthdays. I would have thrown him pool parties with coned party hats and fat cakes and lots of little friends.
'Yes.'
I see the room and I cry. There's too much space around the lone bench, in the middle for violating girls and sucking their babies out. People stand around waiting; cream, blue, white.
'What's wrong?'
'Are you sure you're making the right decision?'
'WHAT IS WRONG?'
It's the room.
'Well, we live in this room, you only have to be in here a few minutes.'
I don't want ... hold me ... take my place ... do something! Head hurts. Fuzzy. Out.

Slowly, I come to, drunk with ache, tears in my eyes. I need to offload pain, hear that it won't hurt forever, my baby didn't feel anything, he understands. I'm so sorry little one who I love. Where did they put you?
I attempt tea and a colourless sandwich on yesterday's brown bread.
No summer birthday parties.

Oh, rescue me from this conspiring chair, fly me to a porcelain white cloud, soft above the world, far from the clinic, the bench.

Another girl leaves, seemingly fine. Am I the only one throbbing, my whole body in mourning? Womb hurt and confused; where is the baby who was only just there? There was such hope for him.

My insides ache, my heart aches, I'm petrified of going to the toilet; the only way to prove I can leave. I waddle, hunched, to the bathroom.

At the top of the landing I'm nervous. What will his face say? I've no control over my own, pink and puffy with life. He's there, concerned, but he feels far away as I'm sinking the indigo depths of my own pain.

In the outside world I wonder, can people tell? We buy a punnet of strawberries, glossy and shouting the colour of life. I talk a lot on the train. Then I don't. My grief kaleidoscopes all around me.

Bearing Witness
Elsa Kurt

Fluorescent lights illuminate every crevice of your newborn face. Still. Pale. Snuggled beneath the white hat and bunny rug you were wrapped in when we were trying to keep you warm, keep you breathing. Keep you alive. I watched you enter the world and I watched you leave, all in the space of a day. But this was the only moment in a thousand moments when I could look at you and actually breath.

I don't count the moment I first laid eyes on you. That was made too slippery by the multicoloured fluids of your birth – red, yellow and brown. And you were purple. Not blue.

Your parents thought you were blue, they'd heard babies could be born an odd colour and weren't worried. Not yet. But I saw purple, hot mulberry purple, and feet that already seemed dead. You looked as though you had no bones.

You made one sound before you went. Not the triumphant newborn wail, but a mewling, small and animal. No one took enough notice, too busy with the louder noises of our own.

Exclamations of relief. Jubilant laughter. Joy entered the room, as we all thought it was the sound of you coming to us. What it really was, was the sound of your goodbye.

I don't count the next time I saw you either. Your skin green and beginning to collapse upon the structure of your bones. You'd been cut apart, examined, and sewn back together. Knowing that beneath your fresh wrappings were the leaking stitches holding you intact, I could scarcely bare to look.

But in that one, extended moment . . .

Your parents sit on the edge of the bed; you nestled into the interlocking configuration of their arms. They look up when I arrive. No words, just sad smiles, an invitation to enter. I don't touch you. You are theirs, not mine, to hold. I am here only to bear witness. I gently place an arm around each of them, my upper body making something of a heart shape.

Together, we gaze upon you.

Smoothest cheeks and wrinkled brow. Delicate new eyelashes. The weave of your woolen beanie. A pilled blanket used on hundreds of babies before you. Waxy white dots sprinkled across the bridge of your nose, flakes of vernix drying on your brow. A tiny downturned crease in your chin. Dry skin in the place where your bottom lip purses slightly.

So slowly, your parents begin to shake. Tears fall without a sound.

The shuddering of your small body as their sobs move through you, you could almost be alive.

As the weeks and months and years fall by, I continue to bear witness to your image. I didn't put my lips to your milky sweetness or inhale your waxy scent. I heard your brief mewl, but didn't realise how sacred it was at the time. I failed to touch you.

All I could do, all I can do, is see you.

So I see you.

The White Sheet
Lesley Beards

Lies and triple lies
I threw the words like spears
back to the officer at the door.
He will be back
He will be back
I cried and slid to the floor.

The white sheet said it all,
His darling face just sleeping
one eye just peeping.
The white sheet is lying
he will wake up
my son has not died.

He did not come home that night
I held his jumper to my face and
breathed his earthly smell.
I did not know from that day on
my future would be hell.
Each day I waited, three months long.

Until the spell was broken and
days became weeks and more,
I waited in the sunroom
watching the closed back door.
I lay on his bed and breathed his pillow
not breathing into it in case I lost him.

I watched him move on videos, we danced
at his sister's wedding, we laughed and twirled
and there was no such thing as grieving.
We had such fun and I watched it again and again.
I heard his voice and closed my eyes pretending
He was in the room, but the soundtrack was deceiving.

He won't come home, I know that now
And my heart will never repair
And bargaining with any gods
Was just a desperate plea
I thought perhaps that some great force
would send him back to me.

Mary Margaret
Marie McMillan

On receipt of the phone call, advising of mammy's inoperable cancer, I must have heard the ghostly gong stroke of Strauss' *Tod und Verklarung**.

'Take me home to my tigin*,' she said, from her hospital bed.

Like a return-to-sender packet she was delivered home – in her blue, feathered hat, maroon coat and matronly brogues – by the ambulance men. Seated on her inclinator, she rose up like a hot-air balloon, until she reached her bedroom. That was the last time I saw her dressed.

We'd always been incessant Blarney stone chatterboxes, not unlike Joyce's Liffey-side washerwomen, but, now, invisible sellotape sealed our lips

'It's a lovely day.'

'It is.'

It's grand.'

Like Hans of Haarlem, we plugged up the dike of our pre-mortem grief with non-sequiturs; inconsequential asides; our mouths stoppering all talk of love, loss, separation, sure the outpourings would have flooded the room.

She was a compliant patient in those final days as the nurse and I trickled teaspoons of tea past her dry lips, inserted suppositories and rolled her over.

'Thanks,' she'd whisper.

'Your mother has fallen into a coma,' said the nurse, when I phoned, one afternoon.

A pre-Christmas conga of cars snaked around the city centre. Not an empty taxi in sight. Finally, I caught a bus going to Dartry, though I really needed to go to Rathgar. Heaving in and whistling out, I couldn't stop my rasping hyperventilations. They were hideous and cacophonous.

To the undoubted relief of passengers, I alighted in Rathmines and walked the remainder of the journey. Rattling and rasping, I arrived home to find the priest giving the last rites.

Too upset to watch, I took my involuntary clattering to my room. A niece brought me a brown paper bag into which I poured my hemorrhaging bawlings.

My shift started at midnight. I'd written a letter of gratitude, listing mammy's goodness, her kindness, her budgetary prowess, her nursing ability, her maternal concerns, her love and selflessness . . . but I was voiceless. The nurse became my reader and intoned my filial gratitude and love in her soft Sligo accent, as we held mammy's hands in ours and listened to her rhythmic breathing.

All too soon, however, THAT rattle started. She sounded like an old goods train shunting backwards and forwards. All too soon, the carriage of her life started decoupling from its terrestrial one, veering off the rails with magisterial puffs of tepid air, soon followed by hesitant ones.

Puff, puff puff. Puff, puff puff . . .

Exhaling languidly, she then puffed twice more through pursed lips – as if, conversely, riding birthing contractions but, more likely, breaching pangs of birth into a new, celestial world.

Softly, she tweaked my fingers with her thumb and forefinger and, silently, signalled her departure from the station marked LIFE.

Orphaned in my newly-minted grief, I finally managed to say: 'Requiescat in Pace.'

* German for Death and Transfiguration – title of Richard Strauss' Op. 24 tone poem.
   * Irish for little house (diminutive)

Braver, Stronger, Kinder

Gillian Swain

How is it that I
Could have lost you. Let you go.
I rocked you inside my soul,
I tried to keep the flame
Alight inside of you
And Failed. I slipped.
Could I have been braver, stronger, kinder?
Could I have mustered more strength
Than it took to say Goodbye?

And if I'd grown from the truth of this
Death
If I'd known the permanence of its scent,
You'd be here now. Perhaps.

I could have loved louder.
I could have fought harder. Perhaps.

I could not keep my grip
Tightened to hold the warmth
That would reveal you.
Out of huddled
Sadness I crept quietly
Wishing for your return,
Drinking the salty
Sorrow that dressed me.
And empty ribs inside both of us
Echoed
Farewells that will never be complete,
Through snatching hands
That held not each other's bodies
Only loss.

Harlequin

Anthony Wood

We sit beside her bed to wait and watch. She lies at rest, trapped beneath a web of wires and plastic tubes. Her mother glances over the top of her glasses at me from the corner of the room. Older, wiser. She says little. A book sits in her lap. On its cover, a rose in bloom hangs like mistletoe above a couple in a passionate embrace. She breathes the book's words like oxygen. Wrapped up in the story, its soft hold soothes.

I visit every afternoon, but, in the morning I chase my thoughts with a brush. In bright sunlight, I stand in front of the easel and stare at a lithe harlequin. I try to trap him with paint but he eludes me and continues, jester-like, to dance in my mind. My portrait takes the form of a cubist Arlecchino. Disjointed, misshapen, deformed. The black background captures the darkness of my afternoon visits. While my subject's unbalanced eyes peer at me through a twisted half mask, I stroke geometric diamonds on his torso with deliberate authority. Each is coloured to match an emotion. Red for anger. Yellow for denial. Negotiated orange. Blue for sadness and cream for acceptance. The skewed shapes form a unique and distorted checkerboard.

In the corner of the room, her mother closes her book and places it on the bedside table. She rustles in a plastic bag at her feet and retrieves some ragged patches of material. From a paper template she cuts the fabric square and, with intense focus, sews precise stitches. The squares form a patchwork of diamonds. A harlequin quilt; a parti-coloured blanket of emotion. I want to wrap myself in it. Our designs are different but the patterns are the same. Her squares are precise, measured. Mine are chaotic, inconsistent and lean into each other. It is the same irregularity that flows through my entire being.

There is a knock at the door. My harlequin thoughts turn a deft somersault and await an entrance. Il Dottore – the doctor – enters with a swoosh. He performs some checks and, like a prophet, delivers the news.

'There is no change. Nor will there be.'

My harlequin thoughts twirl and gyrate. The scene is comedic. A prank devised to gauge my reaction. With a flourish, the doctor leaves. We sit in a silence punctuated only by beeps from a bedside monitor. Her mother ploughs a deep furrow in her brow as she stitches another square. The quilt reminds me of my painting. Tomorrow I will hang a diamond from the corner of my Arlecchino's eye.

The Maxi Taxi

Janey Runci

We're on the nature strip in front of the house in Neerim Road, Sam in his wheelchair, me holding the handles. The yellow maxi taxi has come, late as always, but it's here. The driver gets out, smiling and apologising.

Sam is irritable. 'It's no good.' He snaps the words at me and then turns away.

'It'll be good when you get there,' I say. I'm the one who's persuaded him to go to the gym, to try things, to try and believe that it is possible to live a life when you've become quadriplegic.

'It's not even the right taxi.'

'It might be okay.'

Sam glares at me.

The taxi driver looks sturdy, if a bit on the short side. The last driver had trouble getting the chair up the ramp. The taxi driver smiles and gesticulates as he lowers the ramp. He's proud of his ramp but I can see that Sam is right. It's the same as the last one - not quite wide enough for the wheels.

The driver tries to push the chair up the ramp, his face contorted, one wheel of the chair teetering on the lip of the side. 'Be okay, sir, be okay, lady', he keeps saying, but half way up the ramp he gives in and edges back slowly, easing the chair down. He parks the chair on the nature strip. He says he can adjust the ramp.

We wait while the driver does things to the ramp with tools. Sam mutters to himself and swears.

'All right now!' The taxi driver is smiling again, but his hands rub together nervously.

'Give me the chair,' he says, and then, somehow, I have stepped back, my face turned away and the chair rolls. I dive towards it. I lunge but the chair keeps rolling.

'Grab it!' I scream, and the driver looks up shocked from where he's turned to do something else to the ramp and the chair rolls right back and then tips and Sam's head hits the concrete, jarring the earth, the universe.

Cars pull up and men appear and somehow we get the chair righted and Sam tells the men he is okay and they help get the chair in the taxi and they all drive away.

I walk back through the gate, up the path, through the front door, down the passage and straight out to the back yard. I stand there and stare up through the bare branches of the liquid amber tree. I open my mouth to howl. I stare at the sky. I think suddenly that this is prayer and I don't know why. Not words, not a god. Just the sky above, all over, my mouth open to the sky and nothing in between.

The Earth Turned Over
Phillip Radmall

The sound of the tractor mower is a numb rattle of metal
somewhere way out, dumbed by the broad, heavy lie
of the turf across the down and upslope of this place's heft and fall;
a far noise blurring into the sense of passing day.

All along the hub of my high standpoint are ranged
long, mannered rows of small stone slabs and plaques, bedded in tight,
square to the bevel of each dug plot, each edged lip and flange
yielding to abundant grass. Everything tended well and right.

This is an intervention in the dress of death;
a tidy, fine couture arranged around; neat ties and bows
of careful plantings, soil tucked and smoothed. This is not the rough,
sore agony of hurt, the mess of something wrong on show

like I saw in a once living body, shrunk and shredded
into loose clods of flesh, its bones gone black, barely feeling
its own failing, waddling from a bathroom to another bed
the last time to sleep in, helped and bundled, peeled

of clothes into the final familiar warmth of sheets
used to the lie of better skin, of good skin pressed against my skin
and made whole there with me. It is what the mind still creates:
the earth turned over, the disturbed mess within,

chunks of life roughed up and mangled, as if the tractor's drone
is of it churning up the turf now, upturning line and groove,
the beds run through, the lawns unlevelled, bunkered, unhoned
back to the raw dishevelment they maybe should be, a way to prove

the treachery of flesh, to expose in this neatness what cannot be neat.
So I come to you in your earth, your rest, your measured plot of ground,
to discover its proud intent undone by what the memory repeats,
go home to grieve not over what is lost, but what's still found.

Grey Matter
Rebecca Niumeitolu

When I found you out
in the paddock that quiet afternoon,
perched on your stool,
leaning
against a charred stump, bloodshot
lips curled back, jaw flung open
as if to laugh the purple sky,
I felt relief. Too long
had you been a stray
collecting pebbles down by Lover's Lane,
limbs petrified, ingrown with forget;
chasing red bullets up and down anthills,
till clarity like a web
could only be caught
with an angled light.

>How you would cry
>to the white limbed
>to send you home –
>those widow making
>sirens who tied your tongue
>in a unison black
>thud –
>they sacrificed their smooth trunks
>to the south winds
>that carried you.

I see you there,
still,
eyes rolled blissfully
back to the northern hills
which safe keep memories, at last
let out from that shattered cranial vault.

Inertia
Rhonda Wilson

Caroline, her oldest friend, one of the few she had yet to alienate, dropped by. They made stilted, tiptoe conversation over coffee and Arnott's Assorted. Caroline said they should get together for lunch. Soon. She agreed.

'Ring me,' said Caroline.

'I will,' she said.

But she didn't.

Her husband suggested that maybe it was time to do something with Adam's room. Turn it into a study, another guestroom or, even, a whole-family entertainment centre. What family? She thought.

'Go ahead,' she said.

But he didn't.

Instead, he brought home a collection of travel brochures on luxury cruises, 'swingers' bus tours and DIY backpack and rail pass treks and, for a while, it was better. They spent a whole week of evenings going through them. Plotting and planning; dreaming and designing; and deciding they would go to the travel agency early the next week.

But they didn't.

She held the handset up to the light and inspected it for smudges, cupped it gently in her left hand and polished it with the soft cloth and, finally, placed it back in its cradle.

'Now ring, damn you!'

But it didn't.

They had always vowed that they would enjoy their 'empty nest'. They had lives and interests, and when their sons had flown out into the world there would be no time for lamentations and breast beating; they would be too busy having adventures of their own. They were sure it would make their relationship even stronger.

But what would they do . . . if it didn't?

Grieving for my mother
Jena Woodhouse

Grieving seldom comes clean
from the bone,
though women who keen
sublimate the mundane
in their terrible song;
but for those such as I
there's the gangrene
of action elided
and gestures betrayed
into stasis; journeys
deferred, and lines
never spoken, except
in rehearsal
rooms of the brain.

What is not named,
never done, left unsewn
must somehow be pieced
into something I own:
a mendicant gown
or the ghost of a shawl
she once wore as a statement
of undisclosed pain.

My Mother Died
Lorraine Chapman

Grief has invaded me,
Eating away at my guts,
Squirming like a fat snake lodged in a drain pipe,
Slithered in unseen and unwanted.

Waves of shock and disbelief arrive,
Build to a torrent of thrashing anger by the need to blame,
Bit by bit the rage subsides and hopelessness slips in,
Then ever so slowly, acceptance quietens the fury.

The serpent of grief relaxes,
Shrinks a little and is released from its prison,
The cell is empty now,
Until gratitude arrives, like a sliver of sunlight to fill the void.
Thank you for being my mother.

Grieving the Double Helix

Magdalena Ball

They stood together in the sepia photo I found while cleaning out my mother's things. He was young and handsome, crisp and confident in that way of immigrants. His wife was small and pretty, leaning one hand on his strong shoulder and one hand on her middle boy. His three children (soon to be four) were well-dressed and good looking. He had moved beyond the oppression of his childhood, had graduated from the weedy downtrodden boy his father would sometimes hit, to an untouchable man. He had travelled far from that boy, grown into this life. He was in control and, in this country, he felt sure he would prevail, using his freedom to give his family a bountiful life. This new world would hold him up, laud him, lead him forward towards the greatness he felt in his bones.

She, on the other hand, weighted with prescience and the child growing in her womb, curled her body slightly in readiness for the future. She knew what was ahead of her and though she'd be able to make extra money reading tea leaves for others when her husband was too drunk to go to work, she took no pleasure in her gift. She felt the full weight of time in her bones, felt the impending grief of her children, who, like her, would bear the brunt of their father's failure written in thumbprints on their skin. She pretended to smile but the melancholy already showed.

Like all grief, the pain would change, evolve, come and go in greater or lesser waves, moving through time and space. This was no transient emotion. Her grief was so deep it had become part of her DNA, spiralling its way through the generations she'd mothered. That grief, driven by her husband's violence and self-loathing, became a seed of shame that grew, in the many years to follow, into fear, cancer, death. It became an evil bigger than the man itself, a force surging through generations.

In the centenary of that moment, captured in silver gelatine emulsion, she returns, her dark eyes soft with love. On her lips is a song, sung in the rich timbre of her mother(s) tongue. 'Mekhile' she sings, as softly as breath, as subtle as the wind in the trees outside the room. Through the cycles of her grief she sings of what has been lost and found, of beauty and pain, of death and, above all, of compassion. Her voice opens windows she kept closed through her life. 'Forgiveness' is her song, while I look the monster in the face and see only the man, his dreams intact. Through the mist of my own grief I sing along with her, not to change the past, or diminish the power of the hurt. I accept those things which make me who I am, for I am as much him as her. I sing 'moykhl zayn', harmonic frequencies moving beyond time's arrow, in order to forgive myself.

Grieving Hamish
Rachel Noble

Our beautiful surprise was born on a balmy summer's night. The kind of night where the sheets stick to your skin and you thrash around in the thick air trying to catch your breath. When the obstetrician placed my son on my heaving chest at 3.30am, I gasped at his beauty.

'He's far too beautiful to be a boy!' I said. The obstetrician and midwife chuckled and I stroked his beautiful soft head. We called him Hamish.

Hamish joined our bustling family like he was always meant to be there. We just didn't know we needed him. He was the yin to our yang, his zen-like countenance forcing us to stop and drink big gulps of air. As he grew, the joyful giggles bubbled out of him and we stood mesmerised, charmed. As with all big families, the crescendo of chaos would hit early evening and, in the midst of it all, I could feel eyes on my back. I would turn and meet his glorious baby blues across the room; an invisible cord, binding us always.

At 20 months he was wrenched from life in a drowning accident, so traumatic I cannot recall it without wanting to tear the skin from my arms, scream until I'm hoarse, sob until I'm dry. He left us and we recoiled from life, unable to face it without him. The sun shone too bright, the days were too long and we were left, bewildered, bereft, alone.

The first night, the five of us curled up together in our inadequate bed and whimpered, unable to fathom the massive depth of pain we were in. We clung to each other, trying to ignore the heavy thud of our broken hearts. We tried to draw the curtains on life, livid the world kept turning, but every day it knocked on our door, gave us food, made us tea, held us. The love kept coming and gently, persistently reminded us to live.

Eventually we uncurled our wasted bodies, stretched our limbs and learned to crawl. After some time, and many stumbles, we took our first steps. Today, we walk and have even managed the occasional run, grateful for the wind at our backs. Despite our progress, the grief is constant; woven into our souls and etched on our hearts. We have wrapped the memories of our beautiful Hamish like cloaks around us, keeping us warm in the harshest conditions, keeping him close.

Hamish never leaves us. He is always there. When we fall, he picks us up and, when we rise, he holds us there. You'll see him in our smiles and in our tears, in our triumphs and in our despair. Grief knows no time nor space. It has no height or width or definite shape. It has no boundaries, no edges, yet it is constant. Just like our love for a little boy called Hamish.

Babe of Me

Margaret Polacska

Babe of Me,
Today your first cry should have erased the pain of labour.
Your first breath should have filled your lungs
and turned your body rosy pink.
The midwives should have placed you on my breast
so I could nourish you, protect you.
The delivery room should have been filled with loved ones overjoyed
by your arrival into our world.
Today our dreams should have come true.

Instead I sit here, empty.
Your absence replaced by something dark
that is hard to shake off.
I stand in ill-fitting shoes that belong to someone else.
This is not the life I expected to live.
I want to wear the shoes that mums wear
when they chase their children around the backyard.
I want to chase you Babe of Me
Not just in my dreams, but in my life.

Votive

Jane Symonds

Against your dying, I lit
candles by proxy in distant cathedrals, comforted somehow by
flames that burned so far away, beneath
the loving eye of lives already lived.

Yours was the old God of such
unyielding might, such
flawless lines, such remembered grandeur.
For your eternal destination, you looked back to
times you hadn't seen, and maybe
I longed to light your way

Yours was the God of answers, never
questions, but I was full of them: angry little heathen who worshipped
at the altar of reason, laying
obstinate obscenities at the feet of
so cruel a power

Mine was the inherited God of
insidious guilt and gnawing doubt that ate away
your stone foundations. While your God demanded
only service, I demanded of mine explanations
and justifications. I made pleas to my God of understanding; I struck matches
off my agony and fed the fire with my rage
and I lit tiny lights in places where I had been
happy, storing up warmth for a future
without you, when I would have to
relearn joy

I never saw them go out, those candles I lit for you: never saw them
extinguished as you were when you lay empty on your
hospital bed, never saw their final wisp of being float away to seek
their gods, and I choose to believe
they never did

The Northerly

Andrea Lagana

I hate hospitals. Most people do, I guess. There's not much to like about them really. They smell of fear and hope. Of death. Of life. The small waiting room is crowded and brightened by harsh florescent lights. Family, friends, strangers, and long-forgotten faces. There's too much going on around me. I am silent. It's my turn to go in.

I squirt the antiseptic gel on my hands and rub it in. It makes me feel cold but at least I can feel something. I keep rubbing well beyond the time it takes to absorb. I know this will be the last time I spend with my cousin. I am buzzed through the automatic door. I walk into another world. The Intensive Care Unit. It looks like the size of four basketball courts. The ceiling is high. The blue-tinged light is dim and ominous. It should soothe me but it doesn't.

I don't want to raise my eyes and look around. I can feel the suffering in this space and it overwhelms me. My sandals are silent on the floor as I walk towards my cousin's cubicle. I'm floating. The curtains covering the floor-to-ceiling glass room dividers are duck-egg blue, along with the sheets. I walk past the bed, go around to his left side and take his hand. It feels too cold. The pulsing beep of the life support machine is the only steady sound.

I tickle his forehead and my finger-tips start tingling. His head is hot. I talk to him. A lot of people want to come in here so I'm not meant to stay too long. But I don't want to leave him. We grew up together and I can't bring myself to walk away. My Auntie is approaching, along with his sisters and brother.

'I've got to go,' I say. I lean down and kiss his shoulder. I tell him I love him as I gently dab his tears with a tissue. I let mine roll. Silently. I slowly make my way out.

I open the door to the waiting room. Eyes are upon me. I walk past without speaking. I need to get outside. Down the long hallway, turn right, and down two flights of stairs. The foyer is wide and vast. There are too many people. I've got to get to the exit. The light is shining brightly through the glass doors far ahead of me.

Hold it together, keep it inside. The emotion is rising like a tidal wave.

I make it out. The hot northerly wind hits me in the face and pushes air into my lungs. I can breathe – sort of. I've got to get to the park across the road. The green grass and towering trees beckon for me to take comfort in them. I'm holding on but the feeling's too strong. I let myself feel it. I walk into the park, sit down on the grass and cry.

Dog Bite
M.J. Reidy

'Dog bit me,' I say, showing the receptionist the train track of teeth marks.

She studies my arm, stares up at me. Catches a cough in her hand.

'Medicare card?'

She punches the numbers into the computer, stealing sideways glances at my arm.

When she hands the card back I trace my finger over the long singular line. It's like I'm learning to read a new Braille for single, part-time Dad's.

'Seeing that new counsellor are you? The woman over in Lang Street?' she says.

'Ah... yeah.'

'We had a tiger bite last week. The week before, a goanna attack. The doctors don't know how to deal with it. She's created a whole Noah's Ark for the Bereaved.'

'Good for business though, right?'

She frisks the lapels of her jacket so they stand upright around her ears.

'Look, I lost my husband last year,' she says, her voice turning quiet. 'Try crocodiles. Problem with dogs is everyone's got an opinion on how to discipline them. You can't discipline a crocodile.'

'Thanks for the tip.'

The doctor ushers me into the room with his bowed head. I show him my arm. He grunts and pushes a script into my chest.

'Valium. 5mg.' He raises his eyebrows into umlauts. 'It'll put the dog to sleep. If that fails, tie the damn dog up.'

At the counsellor's appointment, I ask her if I can tether the dog to the chair. It's pacing the room, sniffing her stockings. They're black see-through numbers with bows up the legs, as if she's growing a second skin against the world.

'When I said to visualise your grief, Andrew, I think you took it too literally. But, it's understanding, given your circumstances....'

'I've learnt me lesson, Doc. From the bite, I mean. I should've pushed my weight into the dog's mouth so it'd let go, not pull away. Just made the pain worse.'

'Look, all I'm saying is if you don't own your emotions, Andrew, they become unreal. You need to talk about them. Perhaps we need to assess you for an adjustment disorder.'

The timer on her desk shrieks. I get up to leave, offer my hand out to shake. She looks at it warily. It's like the silent code of plumbers - never to shake hands with a client after you've been elbow-deep up a drainpipe in their shit.

'Sorry about the mess.'

'The stages of grief are messy, Andrew. No need to apologise.' She places her hand on my shoulder.

'Nah, I don't mean that. The dog's urinated on the carpet.' I point to the wet patch near her chair, rising up like a hidden island through the carpet.

I get into the ute, decide not to tie the dog to the crossbar. I let him run wild for a bit. I can see him in the rear vision mirror, snapping at motorbikes, trying to swallow Taragos and their instant families wriggling over the back seats. Biting at something invisible in the wind.

Loss of Intimacy
Desney King

It's almost two and a half years since my life was transformed by a brain stem stroke. I can no longer work, drive, socialise or sit or stand unsupported for more than a couple of minutes – my bed has become a dear and familiar place of solace.

I was 60 when the stroke hit – sitting at my desk at home, engrossed in editing a manuscript. I'd already done some creative writing of my own that morning and been for a power walk around my leafy suburb.

There's so much I've lost – I've not been into the city, nor seen a beach, a campfire, the bush, the inside of a restaurant, the inside of a theatre or the opera house. I've not been on a ferry, nor a road trip, nor a holiday. And yet about those losses, surprisingly, I feel only a gentle sadness. I know the feeling isn't grief, because it's not lonely – I can talk about missing these things without my listener feeling hideously uncomfortable.

But, in recent weeks, a greater loss has threatened to overwhelm me; a slow, deep, profound grieving has stirred and swirled, catching me by surprise and unsettling my typically calm emotional and mental state. I've realised that some of the people I've held dearest for decades are slipping away from me. And it's this gradual loss of comfortable intimacy that has hurtled me into the desperate loneliness of grief.

I cannot make people come to visit me; cannot force them to phone just to yarn about what's happening in their daily lives. If I tried, the artificiality of the contact would undo any sense of ease and true connectedness.

So why don't I phone them? Well, sometimes I do. Not very often because I remember how busy a working life in the city keeps people. Even my attempts at this kind of contact are dwindling because my dear friends are too busy to talk for more than a few minutes, if at all. I feel the urgency of work, or socialising, or other people tugging at them; their awkwardness in wanting to end our conversation without hurting me or being rude. But the intimacy of close friendship is sustained by frequent sharing. A 15-minute chat once or twice a year can only sketch in broad details.

Recently, I've tried talking about this to a few carefully selected people – not those I feel so painfully separated from. They've been understanding, wonderfully supportive. Yet afterwards, my grief has felt deeper, the silence of my solitude more intense.

This morning, finally, I've come face to face with what I know from long ago: that grief is an anguished inner landscape that I must navigate alone; that the journey through it is long and often feels unbearable. And yet I know, also, that over long swathes of dark time, my grief will soften; become less relentless, less pervasive.

Slowly, light will filter in, bringing with it bright glimpses of my newly configured world.

Memories of the Mountains
Elizabeth Sutherland

This is how I like it,
This is my kind of perfection;
Just me, the trees and the moon.
Sweet, silent bliss,
All sides surrounded by you.
Why must it always end too soon?

At the beginning of my forever
A picture of hope was shaped like you
As day after day, moon after moon
Crossed our paths, it didn't flicker.

And now it's been pulled away,
Gently tugging over the months gone by
To be sucked in a dizzying tidal rip
Insistent on stifling the breath out of me

Time that wasn't mine, it was never yours.
To exist amongst the buds of innocent faith,
Proven right will forever be wrong.
There's not much left of me with you gone.

Are You There?

Karen McRae

If I should pick and unpick my way across
torn dreams spun tight over long years,
if I collect the fragments and bones and artefacts
and examine them diligently
for signs and omens,
is it enough?
Shall I find you again?

If I should search the wide, wild world,
from the withering Sahara to the swarming Amazon,
If I salt the lakes with yearning tears
and pepper the roads with tender promises,
until all my breath is ragged
and I am wracked with pain,
is it enough?
Shall I find you again?

If I should aim for the distant speck on the violet horizon,
if I should run true and straight towards you,
if I walk an extra mile or two in someone else's shoes,
in everyone else's shoes,
If I am fast and bold and faithful,
If I am brave and strong and good,
is it enough?
Shall I find you again?

Are you there?

A Consequence of War

Burt Candy

1942
'Dear Val,

Well, darling, just a few lines to let you know that all is well and I am thinking of you and the baby. None of us knows the trouble ahead but I would hate to die before I had a good crack at them. This, darling, will be the last letter I can write before leaving but I will write again at the earliest convenience. I hope to be back with you and the baby in the near future.

    Lots of love,
    Your husband, Bert.'

The Japanese forces had moved down through the Malaysian Peninsula and were attacking Singapore. Australia had decided to send troops to counter-attack. Little did they know that circumstances would change dramatically before these men reached their goal.

In distant England, Winston Churchill made a rash decision. He ordered the troops in Singapore to surrender. When Bert and his fellow soldiers reached the Singapore wharves they were informed of Churchill's determination. The next day they lay down their arms and surrendered to the Japanese without firing a shot.

The irony of this is that, after the war, the Japanese General in charge of the Singapore siege confessed that he would have lost any counter-attack as he had been bluffing about the capacity of his forces. Churchill's decision had been premature.

Along with thousands of other Australians and allies, Bert was consigned by his captors to work on the Thai-Burma railway. It was to be used as a supply line for the Japanese troops pushing towards Australia. The conditions that these men worked in were truly atrocious. Hundreds began to fall by the wayside and either died from illness or were executed when they were unable to work.

1943

There was a knock on the door. A telegram boy handed Val an envelope. With trembling hands, she tore it open, although she already knew what it would say.

'It is with deep regret that I have to inform you that Private Albert Ellis has died from malnutrition in a Japanese P.O.W. camp in Thailand. My sincere sympathies, Minister for the Army.'

A baby cried in the background.

I was that baby.

Today

I learnt of this story from my mother. She carried her grief with her until her untimely death at the early age of 40. I still carry the scar on my soul today and find it impossible to forgive Winston Churchill.

The Shape of Life
Holly Bruce

I am always, it seems, the corner in a solid circle; square peg, round hole.

Soft powdery warmth, the fold and roll of velvet skin, the dome of a feathered fragile head; muslin wraps a bundle of cherished creation.

I ache for the unattainable; a slow hot drip.

I have endured labour – the pain morphs way beyond the explosion that inevitably marks the end of a miraculous forty weeks – elementally it enters my cells and muscles, and makes a home there. It circles and sinks teeth deep, during Shower Teas where discussions of sleep and feeding routines cause it to writhe hotly within the contained space of my skin. It pulls and twists with envy, I fight to control, at the sight of burgeoning prams and newborn cries. Stretching laborious limbs, it kicks – hard – against the sight and song of playground antics, squeals of toddler joy or indignation. It rears and rips when exposed to questions, intrusive verbal probes – spike and prod; a continual return to the same torn flesh.

Surrounding my longing for this little being, is a cloudy miasma; the leak of my loss. At the door of the show, I have no ticket. Awkward shuffles with etiquette, I am overlooked. It is, after all, really, about the kids. The periphery of the circle is never ending, demarcation deepens. Elbows and shoulders fence my entry, actions exclusive.

There is the talk of preschool then, proud insights, flashes of genius and wit.

From the edge of the sphere I look outside the square and leap into a fresh start where predictably the talk stalls and staggers under the weight of my barren being. The labour pains reassert, unfurl like a infant, and flail fists into my heart.

Time blurs, melting the edges a little; children grow. Then weddings and, of course, grandchildren. The reedy mewl of loss reawakens no matter that I have spent years tucking it in, cajoling it to sleep with lullabies.

It appears I have slipped the most common stitch in the weave of female friendship; dropped it. The resultant fabric reveals a circle. A peephole into another world. A pattern exotic and unknown to me; a closed club. Square peg, round hole.

I am a corner I cannot turn.

Diptych: Grief Wakes
Mark Miller

1

Grief pushes back the curtains,
rises from crumpled sheets
into the bathroom mirror,
staring back with its stolen face
of grief, and moves unsteadily
to the kitchen. Grief reaches
into the cupboard for tablets
and a cup, holding them
in trembling hands
before the glare of the window.
Grief washes. Grief dresses.
Grief silently steps outside
into the wish-parade of other faces,
into the stinging daylight wearing
the sun's wardrobe
of a thousand kitchen knives.

2

In the dense hours,
in the tart and wasting dark
when the quartermoon hangs
in the black pepper tree,
shedding only shivers of light
over the wind-skimmed grasses,
blind grief wakes, clasping
and unclasping her cold hands,
running them across
the burr of loss,
and lisps with the wind
over and over
against the ceaseless spume of night
into a morning grey as flint
the vows that were made,
the vows that were broken.

Time and Place Stolen
Jennifer Lavoipierre

Fifteen and furious – she perched on the steps flanked by our two dogs breathing mist into the cloudless cool of a spring early morning.

The Central Tablelands in late September can go either way – ambivalence in temperature, fate and fortune. The chill air hit the heat of my tears as I looked across to my daughter Annie, freshly diagnosed.

Leukaemia the Label, the course of our future and, perhaps, the judge of our past. Fear ascended. The backdrop of scarce greening hills couldn't ease the angst. Nothing could as I tussled with how to juggle this. A tousled son of 13 and a Rock-Solid husband would be my buffers as I stared at 7 months in and out of hospital in Sydney, miles from my paddock. I just couldn't see its scope and sequence back then. No one can and no one should - because sometimes the parameters of how far we must stretch ourselves geographically, privately, are best beyond knowing.

The task, as we faced that Wednesday, was unavoidable. Our wild, beautiful daughter would die if we didn't walk the crazy chemo path. In the earlier hours of that morning, Annie and I had wept in a staccato duet as we hurriedly packed our lives. No beach towels, no play things, but she took her Banana in Pyjamas toy from a thousand years ago - the domestic and the dire in face-off.

The animals nuzzled Annie and I quaffed the last country air preparing for Hospital Smells, sanitized. I would feel like a foreigner.

On the drive to Sydney, concrete encroached in a pox of crusty, grey clusters as we got lost in the harsh angles. On that day, we needed angels not angles. None came.

Blurred moments in a big city hospital were a mélange of emotions. James, the silent son, was compliant; pale in his anxious mind. We were stunned into silent processing in a paediatric oncology ward where sterility was an imperative and I worried at having patted the dogs. Immunosuppression became my stalking sentinel of cleanliness.

I missed our clear skies and learnt that the stars above our paddock could be obscured by events beyond control and that the weather can change in a moment.

Too many nights I slept on the ward by Annie's bed, alert, listening to infusion pumps conversing. When each treatment or crisis was over we bundled our clutter into bags and wobbled away home.

Home was never quite the same, though. Nights were still punctuated with Annie's screams and the days by James' anxiety.

Annie survived the horror time but her feistiness fled for a while. I wondered if it was the agony of events that dented her or the grief of separation from normality.

Today, we occupy our paddock with the same dogs. The view remains over the hills but my outlook has changed.

The journey is never really over with cancer. Peace is pierced by chilling possibility, hovering.

Six Wednesdays
Dionne Mence

He placed his hand gently on my stomach. His other hand held a small cloth, clenched tightly in his fist so as to conceal it from my view. Our silence was interrupted by his coughing. A loud, violent cough, it made his whole body jerk as though someone was shaking him. I bit down on my lip, looked intently at the floor and pretended not to notice as he used the cloth to wipe blood from his mouth.

He breathed deeply, waiting for the tangle of thoughts and emotions inside his head to turn into the words he longed for. He began to apologise. He was sorry for the unseasonably hot weather and the lack of cold water in his fridge. He was sorry that he'd only celebrated thirty-one birthdays with me, he had been certain that he would have had a chance to celebrate more. Most of all he apologised, over and over, that he'd never meet my child.

He spoke of his upcoming journey as though he was going on the train to Sydney for the weekend. He was calm. He was accepting. He tried to joke with me, telling me he wasn't quite sure what would happen when he got there, he thought maybe someone would be checking him in and suggested possible questions they may ask him. Whatever happened he promised me, that if there was any possibility, he'd try to make his way home.

Wednesday morning a nurse called me. Eleven past eleven. She was sorry to be calling me. She'd tried other numbers but I was the only one that answered. She sounded nice, the type who would have offered me a hug if she was talking to me in person.

She told me he was gone.

She was sorry and hoped I would be ok.

Six Wednesdays later she was born. A perfect baby with jet black hair. She made my heart soar with love. I took her home. I fed her. I bathed her. I survived. I functioned. Then I crumbled.

Something threw me to the floor, wrapping me in a cold wet blanket. Each time I tried to shrug it off, its grasp got tighter, constricting my breath until I was gasping for air.

Some days it followed me wherever I went, hanging possessively around my shoulders. Other days it would sit sulking in the corner, tapping me on the arm angrily if I dared think of anything but him.

My daughter soon grew into a toddler with gorgeous curls and hazel eyes. One afternoon, the sound of her laughter led me to her room. She was standing all alone but laughing mischievously as though she had an audience. She threw her head over her shoulder, giggling and shouting 'AHH BOO' repeatedly. I laughed with her and asked her what was making her so happy. She stopped, pointed to his picture and said 'that man'.

I smiled and felt the warmth on my back. Dad had found his way home.

He Opted for Heaven
Kate-Lyn Therkelsen

My son murdered himself. Well, that is what I'm led to believe; that suicide is equal to murder. The act rejects the gift of life and nobody should presume to take such authority upon themselves.

As a parent I instilled in my children a sense of purpose and the knowledge that there was no sorrow that couldn't be healed. Joel was very open about the sudden change in his mind. One day he'd woken up with a head full of crushing turmoil and we were left with only four months to help him. Joel had stopped taking his antidepressants a week before the incident. On the Friday he had enrolled to study nursing at university and was due to fly to America on the Monday for his first overseas holiday. On the Sunday afternoon, the police had found him at the end of a noose.

I had just arrived home from the Sunday morning church service when I was told the news. As those dreadful words fell upon my ears I felt every ounce of hope being sapped from my body. I have never felt so alone as I did in that moment. The guidance that I had always trusted to accompany me through my life felt suddenly absent. I asked myself how something so horrible could happen in my family. After all my efforts, how could my precious Joel still feel so dismissible to this world?

My faith is the pinnacle of my interpretation of the world and all the things that happen in it, however, in mourning Joel I found I had to separate my understanding of his passing from the only system I had ever trusted. I came to accept that the place where Joel had found himself that Sunday afternoon was so dark that even I could not have pulled him out of it.

Alongside my prayers I pondered every principle I have ever believed in. I felt ashamed but I could not deny the presence of doubt in my mind. I grew up in a churchgoing family and the beliefs by which I was raised had taught me that we did not decide when and how we died. But what of my son, who took his time into his own hands? In that moment of finality, when Joel had determined that he had had enough, how had he been so confident in his decision?

These days I maintain a humbling sense of naivety, as it is quite clear to me that I don't even know what will happen tomorrow. The days are still hard, and there is a gaping hole in our family home. I know it will get easier eventually and that there will still be times years from now when it will feel as raw as it does today. Everything I have ever believed in was challenged on that Sunday afternoon. I just have to give it time.

Thylacine
Lisa Jacobson

Pouched dog pacing back and forth,
if we could bring you back we would
and recreate each tiger stripe,
each vertebra, that tight-hinged jaw.

The early photographers believed
our retinae caught what we last saw.
What might haunt you, thylacine,
if science resurrected your corpse?

Frozen concrete, iron bars,
meat gone rancid, shit on the floor.
Four million years in an untamed world
meant freedom could only be bought
by death, the cage door swung open
to the place where dead things go.

Tasmanian tiger, zebra-wolf,
how might you be summoned
now your memory's thin and rare?
Just a few quiet bones and photographs,
this embryo in its formaldehyde jar.

And what else might we seek to restore,
long extinguished, that we now mourn?

Solstice
Suzi Mezei

Who is there to love? I wake and smell winter in my house. It sits in dark corners and creeps like frozen hands inside my clothes. Who is there to love? I walk to a room where a small heater glows orange and she is curled on the couch, sleepless. Orange is the colour of the sun. It is ecstasy. They say dogs are colour-blind but I wonder if she knows. Coco knows more than most. She knows me.

    I lay my head near hers and inhale shampoo and sickness. She is too weak to move, so we just breathe together. I do not speak for the fear of sadness in my voice. I stay mute in case it envelopes us. But she sighs. She seems content to lie together in the early morning.

    Who is there to love? So much of Coco is already behind us. We have relinquished all the parts that made her a joyous being. Now she is dependence and pain. The walking track, the worn, shady boards of the veranda, the serendipitous appearance of cats along the fence; we let it all go. We retired indoors and listened to Leonard Cohen. She didn't complain. I held her jaws apart and forced pills wrapped in liver down her throat. She didn't complain. The vet put needles in Coco's aching body and she cried quietly in my arms. She seemed ready. But her heart betrayed her. It refused to quit. I was shamefully glad. I have held on to what was left.

I pull her tiny body towards me. Death has been too long in coming. Her eyes are different. She hates to raise her head. I bring water in a teaspoon and pour it on her dry tongue. She is swaddled in my favourite jumper and we are watching a documentary about Labradors, just for the sound. Coco loves to bark at tv dogs. But today is the last day. She is silent and exhausted.

    I place her softly on my bed and make the call from the lounge. I like this vet; she's a woman. She has a quiet voice and comes to your home. She carries death gently in a brown leather bag.

    I wet a towel for Coco's nose. Cold water snakes through my fingers. No self-respecting dog should have a dry nose. I pass the hook where her old leash jingles like secret music when you close the door. I move with the efficiency of a tv nurse. But when I enter the room, Coco's eyes are closed.

    Her chest is still. I take the weight of her paw in my hand. She is emptied of dreams and nightmares. She is unburdened. I drop a ragged whisper in her ear. "Thank you." There's no more. Words will not come. And still she accommodates my inadequacy.

I open the window. This world is thick with humans. But who is there to love, that will love me like Coco?

A Constant Absence
Amanda Berry

My mother died at Easter, the month after I turned eleven. For three days I held my breath and hoped. It wasn't until Sunday evening that I finally accepted that she wasn't coming back. As a child, I believed in miracles.

When I was told that she had died I had an overwhelming compulsion to run. I took off barefooted into the evening, through the streets I knew so well, having had a childhood of considerable freedom. I remember ignoring my aunt's worried protests to come back. Fight or flight, I guess.

My father cried that night. The only time I ever saw his tears. Was he crying for her or for himself, knowing the road ahead? He had survived The Depression and World War Two, but single life, a time-hungry business, three young children to care for and lung cancer proved a fatal combination for him five years later.

On her last day on Earth, I sent my mother a flower she never received. I wasn't allowed to attend her funeral. My family dealt with her death by getting on with life. My father's three spinster sisters took turns at living with us; to do the things that needed to be done. My aunts loved me in practical ways with hand-knitted jumpers and home-cooked food. But they were not Peggy.

My mother had married late. She had come from a well-to-do, close-knit Melbourne family. As a young woman she was an elegant, head-turning blonde, too privileged to be much impacted by the hardships of world events. Instead Peg travelled, sailing to Britain, Europe and Canada. She ignored the early signs of breast cancer and coped with her illness in the isolation of a troubled marriage in the middle of Sydney.

My father wed when he was forty-seven. He'd grown up in a large country family, growing oranges on the banks of the Hawkesbury River. During the war he'd been a radio operator in the RAAF, not that he ever talked about it. In his final years, it seemed parts of his life needed obliterating from time to time. As a teenager I knew to hide when he came home staggering and argumentative, fuelled with alcohol.

More than forty years later I grieve for my parents in different ways. Once or twice I have sobbed uncontrollably with regret, forgiveness and pity for my Dad. I know now how hard-working he was and how proud he was of me. His life was ceaseless responsibility and worry.

I think about Mum often. It's a not-knowing longing I feel for her.

A perpetual ache; a void. A wondering of how things might have been. My life changed direction when she died. Her death: a mysterious force that shaped who I've become. The space my mother left has been unfillable but I see her in the blue eyes of my son and remember her in the sweet scent and simple beauty of frangipanis. And I go on, knowing that nothing at all is permanent.

Schism
Suzi Mezei

The summer of my sister's eighteenth birthday, she grew too big for body-surfing at Chinaman's Beach. Suddenly, Mila was bigger than the ocean. She wanted cafes and trams and film festivals. Jervis was no good anymore. She gathered us like relics at The Jervis Bistro, even though we were not yet relegated to her past. I heard the tide crash through the evening darkness as if it wanted to come in and share our table. We passed bottles of cheap wine, not quite believing that Mila would catch a bus early morning and leave us far behind. I refused to make a speech.

'Is this a birthday or a wake?' Tubby Francine's fake cheer cut through the clatter of forks on scratched plates. Her submissive boyfriend carved a supermarket cake. Tubby was the first to score a boyfriend; a spotty-faced trophy. Tubby squeezed my sister's shoulder. 'You go get some, girl,' she squealed. Mila raised her glass above a chorus of giggles. Her mouth was stained pink from cab sav. Rain fell in pin-dots on dusty windows and January felt unbearably cold.

We walked home through a tangle of Scribbly gum and Banksia flowers that hung like lanterns on the foreshore. The scent of sea and forest rose like incense.

'Will you miss this?' I had to ask twice.

'What?' she asked emerging momentarily from her own thoughts. I didn't answer.

We are matching bones in the beast they call family. My father said that pride came before a fall. She's way too cocky. She'll bugger it up. I wished it on her with silent violence. I wanted to say I told you so, to lead her to the beach and talk about what went wrong. But that time remained an unhatched plan.

She packed light. There wasn't much she wanted to keep of Jervis. No need for framed photos. Everything's on Facebook. Mila came to tell me she was on the edge of discovery. 'What's to discover? Trams?' I could not bear her joy. I wanted to say, 'We have the same chin.' Don't forget.

'You can have these.' She laid an assortment of washed clothes and half-used lipsticks on the end of my bed. Bribes. The lights were turned off and I anticipated the sense of longing that would descend at sunrise.

Mila was sunscreen and a harsh whip of ponytail. She was the sound of turning magazine pages and sand on floorboards. She was the part-time checkout maverick who slipped us free chocolates. She was the most surprising girl in Jervis. She was kindest and the most callous.

She appeared like a mirage, showered and sun-glassed, telling me she was leaving. She was ready.

'You coming to the bus?' She whispered. That day, anticipation smelt like mango lip-balm. Departure was the sound of a handbag zip. Mila patted the doona gently. Don't forget.

I sealed my eyes. My father said they're a window to the soul. I stifled farewell. I pretended to sleep.

June's Death
Hazel Barker

The events of that fateful day are seared into my memory. My sister, ten-year-old June, developed a raging fever one night. At seven, I couldn't understand how ill she was.

The next morning, June sat bolt upright, pulling the blanket off me with her abrupt movement. She muttered strange, garbled words and I sat up too, suddenly afraid. Beads of perspiration stood upon her brow, and she seemed unaware of me. Staring straight ahead with a glassy gaze and unseeing eyes, she kept muttering through parched lips.

I slid out of bed and ran to my mother. 'June's looking strange and I can't understand her.'

My parents rushed to June and spoke to her. She lay on her back, her eyes darting all over. What was happening to my sister? I'd never witnessed her so helpless and so sick.

Mum fell to her knees at the bedside and stormed heaven with her prayers. She pressed a crucifix to my sister's lips and kept repeating, 'Merciful Mother, have mercy on her.'

Mum's face turned pale. Her lips moved in prayer. Dad remained strangely quiet, watching June who appeared relaxed. We gathered around. Moments later, she gave a few gasps, her head rolled to one side and she who but a mere twenty-four hours ago bounded with fun, life and energy, now lay still and silent.

I froze at the sight of my sister, so young, so active, stretched out on the bed.

Dad placed a small hand mirror against June's face. His Adam's apple slid up and down. With a look of anguish, he left the room.

His gloom rolled towards us like a damp fog, and plunged us into despair. Mum shut the door and hastened to June.

My sister stared at us but the light had gone out of her eyes. After attempting to close her eyes without success, Mum placed a coin on June's eyelids until they remained closed of their own accord. She kissed her forehead and told us to do the same. Then she fell on her knees beside her.

The hand of grief gripped me, giving a choking, stifling sensation. A lump stuck in my throat. I stole away and threw myself upon my bed, shaking with sobs. A solemn stillness prevailed. The room grew dark, as if a black cloud had passed over the sun.

I felt a hand on my shoulder and turned around, trying to distinguish, through my tears, the figure standing behind me.

'Don't cry,' my brother Bertie whispered. 'June's in heaven, you know.'

His words of sympathy only caused me to break into more frenzied sobbing. He did his best to console me but to no avail. Totally lost, I couldn't survive without June, my constant companion. At nights, I had shared her blanket, her bed and her bodily warmth.

Days passed. Desolation greeted me from every direction. I curled up in bed like a wounded animal and sought solace in slumber.

Overwhelmed, I lost part of my childhood.

Party
Heather Taylor Johnson

37 degrees and fish cakes sizzle on ohs
of oil, the militant egg flip, the glass doors
wide open so you don't know if you're in
or out: in is the teacher's new tattoo
and open illicit affair and out the tradies who circle smoke
and squint into the sun – could be the out crowd
are in, depending on your teenage years.
When I ask about her father she is prepared
(the spatula busy as a magnet over nails).
Yes he is so thin and small
would vomit half a fish cake up
but there are memories of a larger man
resting on the bench in the shed
next to the sander and the angle grinder;
you can see him if you go in there
and close your wet eyes, hammering.
This is what happens. This is what happens.

Husband
Diane Barkas

He was closer to me than water to water

When his year was nearly over
and our holly bush had fruited
Paulie said, I think I'll go now
if you promise to eat your veggies
always wrap up warm in winter
put your handbrake on when idling
turn the water off when changing a washer
don't wear flip-flops when you're mowing
I can go . . . if you promise to remember.

Like Father, Like Son
Fiona Macdonald

You said you would be leaving, but I didn't think it so
A cry for help we'd wondered, but you wouldn't sink that low
The news arrived one morning, but little did I know
You'd made your decision, I screamed a heartfelt 'NO'

The shock set in so deeply, right from the start
To lose a father like this can obliterate your heart
A dense fog appeared that day, one that wasn't easily shifted
I still await that glorious day when it will be finally lifted

A troubled soul you were, yet top of your profession
Who would've thought you'd make this choice, the shock will never lessen
That day my soul was ripped apart, the trauma far too much
How would I recover, from the shock and horror and such

The nights became an abyss of confusion, loneliness and fear
The time it took to begin recovering never really felt near
Little did I know there was a bigger shock to come
How could this be possible, my healing had only just begun

The call that changed my future was one of despair
My only sibling had fallen into the black dog's lair
This one hit me harder, but surely wasn't true
Why would he just leave us, without providing us with a clue

A note was left this time, an explanation we thought
But only three lines later, with sadness we were fraught
He gave no signs or hints of trouble, a loner, we all knew
But busy with his business, an empire he grew

Our joyous mother's day lunch, was merely weeks before
That day he brought us both flowers, which touched me to the core
The last time that we saw him, he must have known his fate
For the gift he left us with, was perhaps to compensate?

To lose these two male figures, the most important in my life
Has left me feeling empty, and rejection and pain is rife
The confusion of emotions never seem to dissipate
But I still have my beautiful mother, a blessing, make no mistake

So now I continue to wonder, when will this fog clear
And return me back to normal, without any fear
Deep down I know that I will never be the same
For I'm now the last person to have our family name

Why

Tania Connolly

I clutched the doorjamb and unleashed a bestial roar before slumping to the floor, sobbing and shaking.

We'd weathered 18 years together – mostly stormy – but John swore he'd never leave me, swore he'd try to be strong for me.

My eyes burned and scratched with each blurry blink. I chanced a glance at the bed and John's lifeless, vacant baby-blues stared back at me. A tidal wave of anger washed through my body. I curled my fists, prepared to do battle and inflict a torrent of physical pain worthy of my despair. My heart hurt. I felt raw and exposed. In that moment I hated him. Hated him for his betrayal, for giving up, for abandoning me. Yet I loved him still . . . deeply. He'd fought hard but remained imprisoned within his demons' poisoned talons. We both knew it was a losing battle.

I sat, hugging my knees, rocking back and forth until my sobs subsided. I unscrunched the sodden note clutched in my hand and heard my son's voice for the last time.

'I'm so sorry, Mum. I know you'll blame yourself but it's not your fault, it never was. You tried to fix me but it isn't possible. Life's too painful. Please forgive me and let me go.'

With tears streaming down my face I crawled, a little stiffly, toward my baby. I kissed his cool forehead, tucked away a stray curl and said goodbye.

The Woman Who Wasn't To Be
Jackie Macdonald

I killed a woman once. Not literally, of course. I metaphorically murdered her; committing her to a heterosexual grave with the realisation I was gay.

But it wasn't a swift, one-action murder. It took years to realise she had to die and at first I was unable to let her go.

You see, this was the woman I assumed I would be: Straight, married, a mother, normal. She was safe, unobtrusive, respectable.

So when I realised her life had to be extinguished, a shower of grief rained down on my spirit. While it might seem indulgent to mourn someone non-existent, I desperately wanted her to live life for me.

In the lead up to her death my closet became her home, a place she hung around, waiting to be slung on like a coat of obscurity when I was feeling vulnerable. Because I never asked to stand out.

Not like in my pre-gay days when I valued all that was alternative, an attempt to rebel, to flip the bird to the status quo. But when difference is thrust upon you, it can strip your individuality, drive you to withdraw, to try to blend, not protrude.

So if I met someone new who assumed masculine at my mention of a partner, I'd run with the lie, leaving them uncorrected, choosing instead the easy façade of my heterosexual persona.

I wore her when I went to visit my nanna, whose extreme religious views deemed homosexuality a sin, a one-way ticket to the depths of hell.

'Not that they can help it,' she'd say, 'They just shouldn't act on it.'

And the woman who wasn't to be came to work with me sometimes. She'd appear for colleagues I knew had conservative values or for those I heard make homophobic quips in the lunchroom.

But eventually frustration superseded fear and sadness. I chose instead to confront the reality of this woman, this supposed ideal, this handbrake on my happiness. And I finally saw her for who she was.

Like many a lesbian before me, she was actually my inner homophobia. The little voice who niggled at my sense of self-acceptance. She told me my wish for fulfilment was undeserving and she reminded me to tow the line in a hetero-centric world. She said I should be her instead of me.

She was a bully who was pushing me into dejection, but I became determined to stamp her into oblivion.

So with each little coming out, the knife twisted deeper. With each claim of confidence, her death came that bit nearer. Until finally I threw her into that grave of vulnerability and stood loud and proud of becoming the woman that I am.

I Grieve
John Hall

I grieve for me, the me I could have been
I grieve for me, the me I have not seen
of things unsaid, of things undone
of things I left unsaid and songs I left unsung

I grieve for who I am, for who I have become
for not just being here, recognising that I am one
One with everything, just part of this sweet life
I grieve because I know the truth, there is no fear or strife

I grieve because I've learned there is no going back
I grieve because I felt such loneliness, such emptiness and lack
I could have had a life so full of play and joy
I should have listened to my heart when I was just a boy

Should have taken the path that I was called to follow
and I would not be sitting here feeling just so hollow
knowing that I've wasted time, frittered away my past
doing things to impress others, not following my heart

Yes, I grieve today, because I feel such pain
chasing earthly pleasures that simply bring no gain
when I could have lived as if each breath were my last
seizing every moment then, not living in the past

My grief is overwhelming me, engulfing me in tears
washing over me, filling me with fears
I'm feeling so alone, so sad I want to cry
looking back on my life, the way it's passed me by

My grief is telling me that I need to change
focus on the present now, let go of my rage
Let go of the past right now, live my life right here
Live my life as if there is nothing left to fear

Focus on the joy I have, the simple joy of being
breath into this sweet moment, here, it is so much more freeing
Grieve not for things I cannot change, grieve not for yesterday
grieve not for friends I've lost, let fear not hold it's sway

Let the sunshine wash my grief away, as it does the dark
Let the present moment cleanse me now, ignite my holy spark
Let the joy of simply being here fill my heart with love
connected to every living thing, connected to above

Tom

Simone Mackinnon

'I want to go riding.' His face was red with determination, his chin on a level with the kitchen counter, eyes staring straight into mine.

'Don't nag, Tom – later'. His eyes followed me as I prepared lunch. He sulked and everyone talked as we ate in the kitchen. His foot kicked my chair.

Exasperated, I gave in. My daughter took him down to the paddock. His pony was bullet proof – or so we thought. A scream, running feet, the worst nightmare. A sunny, windy Saturday turned into a maelstrom of horror.

'Tom's been thrown'. A clap of thunder and gentle horses had turned into manic devils.

He lay in the paddock – gasping. His body contorted, dust on his face, his clothes.

We carried him inside and lay him on a bed, called the ambulance. We stared, told him, willed him to breath. To live. The ambulance came so slowly. Nothing to be done. The afternoon turned into night, two best friends waited through the night with me. We walked the paddock and sat in the kitchen. Until cock crow.

'He's gone,' I said and so it ended and so it began.

The days were grey. People came with gentle faces. I smiled, made cups of tea, wrote letters, put one foot in front of the other. We laid him in the ground, a little white and blue coffin. Hail stones and shafting sleet punished us. Hundreds came, children and adults in bright clothes, they gleamed through the dark of my mind. He would have wanted the bright colours. For many nights I lay with his teddy bear, unable to sleep. I felt the warmth of his red dressing gown as he stood by my bed that last morning. I stuffed the bear in my pocket and carried it with me during the day. He sent me messages, Morse code just too fast for me to read. I saw crosses on his photographs. The messages faded and so did the crosses, they are not there anymore. His sisters grieved in their own way, the eldest never spoke of him again, the youngest put his picture in a frame for my Christmas present. We gathered everything of his together. I went to the school, his teacher cried. They put posters up in his school – ones he would have liked – with a remembrance plaque. I never could go and see them. We carried on with our lives, school and jobs and the emptiness where once there was four of us, now there was three.

The grey mist cleared slowly and the colours of life came back; the horrors faded when we began to enjoy life again. We laughed. Except on his birthday and Christmas; except when the memories niggle, on bleak Saturday nights. Twenty eight years later and I still turn to look at small, blonde boys in the street. I try to remember his voice. Now there is just an ache, somewhere where my heart should be.

The Art of Grief
Bindy Pritchard

In a matter of days three different people had referred to the funeral as 'the wedding.' The sisters weren't surprised; these things were normal. They sat in the front row of the small crematorium, their shoes lined up like stranded boats, knees pressed in against the other, and drank in the heady perfume of Asian lilies and white roses. Such indescribable beauty brought tears to their eyes, though it was the curtains they were to discuss on the way home.

'Mum would have died at the curtains,' laughed the eldest sister.

'I can't believe the floral fabric. The dead deserve something more respectful. Like velvet.'

Everyone was glad to alleviate the tension with humour. Death must be dealt with in a sensible fashion, the sisters agreed later as they cleaned out their mother's cupboards. They filled the charity bags with a lifetime of jumpers, slacks, blouses, shoes and matching handbags. However, when they found the good outfits at the back of the wardrobe they were reluctant to remove them from the special coat-hangers and relinquish their delicate shapes. They recognised the watered silks of family weddings, the navy and cream suit she wore to the first grandchild's christening and the anniversary pleats.

'We must be sensible about this,' urged the older sister who held one of the dresses high above her head, the same way she would lift her children's baby clothes, imagining their bodies filling out the grow-suits like budding cacti. But she couldn't inhabit her mother in these dresses now; at the time of her death her body had held a sparse fragility.

'Think about those poor people who'd love outfits like these,' suggested the younger sister and so their decision was reached.

'Life must go on,' they said to each other as they cooked meals for their father, freezing them into single portions. 'Acceptance,' they preached to their friends over coffee mornings. One night both sisters dreamt of their mother. She was as small as Thumbelina and they carried her around in their pockets as if she were a loose pencil. The older sister puzzled for days about the dream.

'What can it mean?'

'Nothing. It's normal.'

The older sister wasn't so certain though. She had never spoken about the night of their mother's death when the undertaker's assistant arrived and she was shocked by his youthful, schoolboy appearance. Not wanting to upset him, she tried to make the experience as easy as possible. She covered the scant, bird-like body in an apricot-coloured sheet; smiled and talked about the arrangements with a steady, natural composure. She almost wanted to give the boy a tip for his troubles. But what she wanted to do more than anything was to follow the draped bundle he carried down the stairs; follow it all the way to the silent hearse and then through the grid of neighbourhood streets, clutching onto the apricot fabric as if it were her mother's hems, and she were a child again.

Coming and Going

Karina Quinn

The thing is I had never seen death up so close.

On the plane I held the breadwarm body of my baby
and tried to see the ground.

I hoped you would wait for us, for him.

What did I know about you? What would I lose
when you were gone? A God Bless on the phone
two or three times a year. The memory of finding
you, the sound of your voice recognising mine.

A grandmother I had known by name
become real. Somerset accent,
a fine gold cross around your neck ready
to be clutched, a poodle
that guarded you from table tops.

We landed. I found my sister by the baggage carousel,
was glad for her glossy lips, the diamontes in the arms
of her glasses, her shine against my Melbourne black.

We drove Canberra's wide roads and she
said 'Granny's very poorly', and 'it might be a shock'.

My baby grabbed at sunlight while I tried
to make myself ready.

But the thing is I had never seen death
up so close so I wasn't. Ready.

For the greyness of your skin.
The cavern of your mouth.
Your gusting stale breaths.

They said your bones were breaking
as you lay. They had not given you food
or drink for days. I sat and held your hand,
your large boned brittle fingers twitched.

I held my baby close and introduced you. I put his hand
in yours and saw his hermit crab fingers scrabbling over your palm.

One arriving, one leaving.

You moaned, then sighed with your heaving
and rattling chest. He wriggled and kicked.
It would be days yet, but we could not stay.

Back on the plane I could still smell old
saliva and saline. Back on the plane my baby
sucked, and held my thumb in his fist, and slept

Don't Shut the Door

Mireille Bucher

The door stayed open for five days this time.

I just had a feeling, you know? That it would be longer this time.

There is nothing special about the door and the paint is starting to peel. I started picking at it the last time the door was shut. I started to pick in the shape of the moon but the paint got stuck under my nails. I just kept picking.

No one goes in there except me but only when the door has been opened. I rearrange the toys, open the window, just a little, so it doesn't get too cold in there. Bring a new book to the front of the shelf so there is something new to look at. *The Magic Pudding*. Yes. I will read that tonight.

The linen needs to be washed so that it is fresh and give the floor a quick vacuum. You don't want the dust to build up. It could irritate breathing at night time. I don't think I need to dust the shelves. It was only recently that I did them, but, oh, hang on, there is some dust over there. I will just blow it away.

Could someone please just answer that phone! I should have put it on silent. Whoever it is will leave a message. I might call them later. Or tomorrow.

The door was open for sixty four days last time. Even had a chance to see the Magnolias bloom. Never did see them fall.

I slept in there last night, on the old chair, listening to soft music from the mobile and just watching it going round and round and round. I woke with a blanket on me. Someone must have put it on me during the night? But no one is allowed in here! I'm so cold though.

I'm going to have to shut the door now.

I have to remember to take the dirty cups out this time. There are a few of them. Mould. Only when I leave the tiniest bit of coffee. Well, depends again on how long the door is shut, I suppose.

Apparently this time, also, just wasn't the 'right' time. I don't think I can wait much longer for the 'right' time anymore.

I'm lying just outside the room, on the floor.

My head hurts. I hurt.

It's a bit cold but I can see the light shining through the crack just under the door.

The door is shut.

Warmth

Lisa Fritz

I take his withered hand in mine. It is cold now. My whole life his hands have warmed me. When I was a child he used to take my hands in both of his just to keep them warm. Like a winter blanket, cosy and comforting. Always safe. Always sure. I can't bear that they are now as cold as mine used to be. I lay my head gently on the crisp white sheets of his bed but I will not let go. I cannot let go. If I do I fear I will fade away, turn into a vaporous mist and slowly dissipate into the atmosphere.

So I hold on by remembering. Starting with the little things, like coffee drops in his beard, and the smell of cigar smoke in the evening. With words, too, and gestures like his little shoulder shrug. I remember his eyes that held as much warmth as his hands. I even recall how his teeth clenched when he would become angry at the teenaged version of me, and how he would tell my best little friend and I to 'stop that incessant giggling!' when we were just kids, and how we all laugh about it still. Well . . . there is no laughter inside this fog I have become.

Slowly I look up, and, frightened by the finality of it, I find his face. It's lack of expression is the harshest goodbye I will ever experience; and holding his hand is my only anchor. The fog that is me now gathers and becomes a swollen black nimbus and drop by heavy drop I start to rain. Each drop full of memories. Heavy with gratitude for a life well given.

He has shaped me since I was born and I am afraid I don't know what shape to be now. But I do know that I have to let him go. He has somewhere else to be. And I have to take my mist, my fog and my cloud, and reshape it. Draw it all together into something solid again. Something that can laugh and thrive, be whole, and can lovingly take a child's hands to keep them warm.

Vanished
Kate Robin-White

I was eight. He was fifteen. It happened on no particular day. That was almost the most disturbing thing. There should've been something special about that day, some telltale sign but my brother seemed his usual self, right up until he disappeared. Looking back, I think the herald of trouble was this inarticulacy: His mute approach to living. He'd likely run away, the police said; Just as likely, he'd be back soon enough. No one knew anything for sure and I didn't dare raise the questions that consumed me like so many white whales to chase.

Eventually, I came to view my parents as strangers; they were almost animal in their grief. Their eyes would catch at me, following me so I always felt them. My mother often came to me in quiet moments, like when I'd sit down to watch TV or after I'd gone to bed. She'd hang about like a gathering storm until whatever it was holding her together came undone, then she'd cling to me and cry. It reminded me of the women I'd once seen at a Pentecostal service, grasping each other, clawing the air, crying out to Jesus with ecstatic desperation. She drove me crazy; it was crazy – diving into someone's agony that way.

The woman stood in the doorway, her shadow stretched along the floor twice as large as her daylight self. She stood until her daughter fell asleep. The girl seemed twice as small as her daylight self and impossibly fragile. These vacant hours unwound the woman, casting her out of herself so that her shadow seemed her only anchor to the present. At times, she thought she might go on expanding this way forever; follow her son into the nothingness, which had devoured him. She guarded against that fate as her daughter expanded; the girl's limbs sprawled like a starfish.

The woman longed for the peace spread over the child's sleep-warmed cheeks. She crawled into bed beside her daughter and fell into her imagination – once more; she heard her son's mellifluous laughter running through the house, saw the square set of his jaw, dreamt up the suit she'd buy him for graduation. She dared herself to hope that he'd regrow from these excised pieces; each imagined future made more vivid by the rage that asserted itself at dawn.

I felt the future pressed out of me by the weight of my mother's form cutting through the light from the hall. It seemed like someone had replaced the mother I'd known before my brother vanished, and that my new mother was sometimes a ghost but mostly very human – a woman, reaching for faith.

When my brother didn't return, and neither did my old mother, I grew good at pretending. Sometimes, I'd pretend she wasn't my mother at all. That made it easier to pretend I was still asleep while she whispered her prayers into the darkness and gave thanks that she still had one good child, one child who wouldn't leave.

Whitewash
Bronwyn Lovell

In the absence of ocean, she runs deep baths,
pours water into cups, brews.

Watching the tealeaves swirl, she wills the current
to wash away her grief.

Safely behind the bathroom door, steam envelops
her nakedness, mists the mirror,

blurs her image till she is no longer sad or alone. Here,
she can drift among the clouds, pretend

her grandmother still lives, smile at the echo of
faint footsteps further down the hall.

Elsie is shuffling about the house as she always
did—singing softly in another room,

watching the telly, boiling the kettle, watering
the garden just out of sight.

I Think

Sarah Whitaker

'I've met someone else.'

The statement tumbled from my mouth too fast, nerves altering my normally deep voice into that of a stranger. I want to grab at the air, desperately reclaim each word and force all four of them back into the safety of my mouth, unspoken.

Oh dear God, this wasn't as I had practiced. I had been able to change the wording and tone with each recitation, studying my reflection in the bathroom mirror, polishing this mantra. The enveloping steam leftover from the showers heat always managed to soften the harsh cruelty of my task.

I stare at my feet, the sky, anywhere but at her.

My stance falls slightly, curling my shoulders inward. I'm broken.

Of course I had anticipated that silence that would naturally follow an announcement like mine, but her quiet deafens me unexpectedly and the weight of her silence forces me to say more.

'You know I have loved you since I was a boy, Mags. Only you. But the last six years have been . . . '

I frantically search the terrain of my brain for the words. Shit, I hadn't prepared for this part. My pain is soul-deep, but I continue because my love for her is deeper and I owe her this truth.

'. . . Well, they have been lonely. Torture. You must know that . . . '

I fall to my knees before her – my wife of 29 years – barely able to catch breath between my sobs. I plead my case, attempting to free myself from the chains of my guilt and shame.

I tell her everything, every sordid detail, until there is no more to reveal. I have used every tear, my tongue salty and shirt wet. I recline, exhausted, on the grass beside her. Free.

My hand rises to touch her instinctively, as I have done every day in one way or another since we met at 15. My fingers trace the engraved letters of her name on her headstone: Margaret Bannerman – Beloved wife and mother.

'Oh Maggie. I think you'd really like her . . . .'

The Bingo Game
Johanna Emily Gilman

Bingo is played every afternoon at the Midway Nursing Home, a ten cent contribution fetched a dollar prize: the caller calls out the numbers loud and clear.

'Bingo!' Matilda sings out. Her fellow players frown - Matilda has the devil's luck. She won more often than anyone else.

Matilda twitches with pride, five games in a row she has won today.

'Eyes down,' the game caller announces. Again she calls the numbers and the players' full attention fall on the game.

'Bingo!' Fred calls and takes hold of the dollar prize. Matilda screws her face for her luck has betrayed her this time but Fred is pleased he has knocked Matilda off her perch.

Amid the revered game, the co-ordinator walks into the room, she wears a solemn face. The bingo players glare. How dare she disrupt the game with that look - the look that promises some sad news. What is wrong with the woman? thinks Fred. Why would she bring sad news during this time of pleasure? The war with life is over and lost, old age is the cruel victor and joy is desperately needed.

All who live in the nursing home wear the veil of grief, for none are there by choice and Bingo brings great relief from despondency and stress. So why is the darn co-ordinator willing to poison this bit of fun with some unwanted, sad news?

Unaware of the players' annoyance, with tear sodden eyes and lowered head, the co-ordinator places her right hand over her heart and announces that Elsie Brown has passed during the night.

Tom's nostril's flare.

'Course she died. We all know that,' he complains, staring at the co-ordinator, 'She's not sitting in her seat, is she? So where else would she be? Dead! There's no more Bingo games for her to play.'

Death is a common foe in the nursing home. Every week, somebody's number is up. Life has become too precious to grieve over someone else's release from old age. Bingo is the only joy that is left and joy is all that matters: time has become too important to waste on grief and there is another dollar waiting to be won. Her news delivered, the co-ordinator retreats from the room and Jess instructs the caller to get a move on. Max and Jan are eager to get a chance at a win so spur the caller on. The caller, sad that Elsie Brown has passed away, understands these people have their own way to deal with grief and sets her own sorrow aside. She dedicates the next game to Elsie Brown and raises the stakes to two dollars. With clear voice she calls out the numbers. All are eager to get the two dollar win.

'Bingo!' Calls Matilda.

Michael
Ann Blackwell

The specialist called me into his office and just blurted it out. 'Your husband has cancer and has not got long to live.' I wanted to hit him. He had no right telling me this when all I was doing was bringing you in for a checkup. I could hardly breathe.

'But he has pleurisy, his doctor said so,' I cried in vain.

'No, he has cancer and it's rapidly spread to his liver,' he said calmly.

My mind went blank, my body froze, and I could not look at you. The doctor's voice drifted off to a distant part of my brain. He must be wrong. You are only forty-three and have been going to work up to a couple of days ago. You looked so frightened, my love.

One part of me was cool, calm and silently efficient but I had this searing pain ripping through my chest, constricting my breathing. Our three children looked at me with big, bewildered eyes and were not sure what to do. I told them dad was very sick and in hospital but I would bring him home.

I fought to take you home. I just wanted you near me and I felt you would be better off surrounded by your family. Your friends and work had organized everything for you to stay at home, including nurses. You asked to learn meditation with all of us, so that was organized. My anger towards this poor man was extreme. He seemed to be taking up so much of my precious time with you. I convinced myself that you had six months, until I walked out with the doctor and said, 'How long does Mike have?'

'About two weeks,' he said quietly.

I could not speak and rushed to the shed and vomited. I had to keep it together for the kids. No one tells you how to handle this; you just make it up as you go along.

The house flowed with friends and love and I asked your mother and sister to come from England. They were shocked and said they would come the following week and I said, 'No immediately.' I was terrified but you seemed so much happier at home.

You were restless so I got up at 5 am and said I would make you and the nurse a cup of tea. Suddenly you began vomiting volumes of blood. The nurse took over and told me to call an ambulance. My hands were shaking so hard that I could not dial the number. The kids came out looking terrified and I told them you had to go to hospital but that they should go to school. When I arrived, medical staff surrounded you, concerned about a drip in your foot that had come out, not you. I asked them to leave and held you as you drifted into unconsciousness and life slowly slipped away from you.

I screamed for my children just wanting to hold onto them tight, terrified something might happen to them. It was only ten days after being diagnosed. Your mother and sister were at Sydney airport, so did not get to see you. I drifted through the days but felt as though half of me had been hacked away. I don't think I dealt well with my childrens' grief and I learnt to hide my own, deep inside me.

Mike, you do heal again and I can see you now laughing, thinking, 'what a wimp. It's taken her thirty years to write this!'

Everflow
Kimberley Hodge-Freed

When she died,
she didn't even pause to close her eyes,
as if watching my reaction: Grandma died

At sunset a Learjet blazed its busy way
across the summer sky.
And life goes on, no matter how I feel, no matter who has gone.

At sunrise through red eyes,
every moment is absorbed with memories and gladness,
with the terrible, aching, sadness of it all.
And cars drive by and babies cry, and cats beg to be fed,
and all the while my mind mutters;
She's dead, she's dead, she's dead.
But that doesn't change it, so I stagger on instead.

Days get cold with stories left untold.
I miss her knowing look,
and cuddle to my chest her cherished cooking book.
The window darkens - she used to love a storm,
we'd snuggle up together, safe and loved and warm.

One year later and I cry – it's been a while since I last had.
There are things in my life that she doesn't know,
and that makes me sad.
But I do what I do, because I always knew
that this time would come. I'd been told she was old.

Years pass, her clothes look dated in the last photograph.
I dust it tenderly, press a kiss to the glass.
She hugs me from within now, so I am never without.
I gently place it down and smile,
and forget it for a while.

My Journey
Sue Masens

It's a journey I suppose, one I don't want to take but has been forced upon me. First it's the invasion of hospital equipment: a bed, a walker, lifting machine, shower chair, and a contraption that sits over my toilet to accommodate my six foot tall husband with no thought at all given to me. It matters not that my legs swing in the air.

The doctor hands me an orange and a hypodermic syringe.

'Here you go, practice on that,' she says. 'It will be easy soon enough.'

It's not.

Same as it's not easy to fit a catheter to empty his bladder twice a day. Or to slide him around on special sheets to ease him up the bed. But I do, and I dribble moisture over his poor dry lips from a damp cloth, being careful not to touch his sore tender skin. And I sit beside him for hours reading Dickens while he just drifts in and out of sleep to soft strains of Mozart.

The worst part for me is the sense of absolute helplessness. To have to sit and watch the man I love slowly waste away because the law says I cannot help him die. He pleads with me to overdose him to end his pain. I begin to shake uncontrollably and scratch at a red rash I have developed. I steel myself, bottle up my emotions and gulp back my tears. In a choking voice I cannot recognise I say,

'Sorry, love, but I can't do that.' While every fibre within says why not? Why can't I? Instead, I gently tuck a pillow under his poor bony knee, pull a soft sheet over his skeletal frame and turn the light down to a soft glow. We sit in silence. I cannot speak for fear I will scream. He does not speak. He has nothing more to say.

There are a thousand questions running through my mind. How does he feel about dying? Has he anything to ask me? What does he believe now that the end is nearly here for him? Does he believe in God? All these things I want to ask him but my throat tightens and I lose my voice. I can barely keep it together as I nurse him day and night.

The children arrive. They each have a private time alone with him, and say what? They come out one by one and hug me then go off. Everyone battling their own demons and I am left alone again with him and this horror, this never-ending nightmare. I fall asleep beside him, dream of more pleasant times. We are riding horses together along the beach

'I'll race you to Blacksmiths,' he calls and canters off in front.

I wake startled.

He's gone on ahead and left me behind.

Dear Sister

Mary Alys Shuttleworth

Dear sister,
    You have been missing for three days.
    The police were called when you did not come home the morning after the first night; after you did not answer your phone and your friends did not know where you were. There were three of them that came to our door. I kept thinking you would burst in any moment, arms full of papers. You would see us sitting there with clenched teeth and our heads in our hands; see the tight-faced police officers, their expressions grim. You would roll your eyes, call us crazy for overreacting; explain you had been at Bona's like you always were, that your phone had run out of battery like it always did.
    You did not burst in.
    Instead the police officers took notes. We responded to their questions with minute movements of our heads.
    They said we were not to worry; that it had only been a day; that for young people these twenty four hour disappearances were common. You had been gone twenty six hours, but I did not correct them.
    When they left, I made Mum and Dad tea in an attempt to regain some semblance of normality, but it was not as good as when you make it. I know because Dad barely touched his. The heat of the mug left a ring on the mahogany table. No one but me has noticed.
    You have been missing for three days. The police no longer tell us not to worry.

Dear sister,
    You have been missing for five days. The police are no longer optimistic. Those two days, they tell us, make all the difference.
    Dad is not going to work. Instead he drives around streets you usually walk down. Sometimes he calls out your name but you never answer. Mum has not eaten for days. Aaron has not slept. Your cat sits on your bed, guarding it, waiting for your return.
    I did not know how easily a day could become an infinity. The minutes creep past us in a slow trail of trickling time. None of us are talking. Sometimes your cat yowls in the night.
    The people who love you are stagnant.

Dear sister,

People talk to me as though you are dead.

Dead people get caskets and funerals; they get eulogies and flowers – but you will not get these things, for you are neither living nor dead. You are missing.

The police came to speak to us again. They said even fewer people could look for you now. Dad put his head in his hands and wept. Aaron shook. Mum pulled out a fistful of hair.

It has been eleven days.

Dear sister,

If they find you now, we will no longer be able to have an open casket funeral. You will be too far gone.

You are still missing, and there is nothing we can do.

Diploma of Grief
Nicki Reed

It's two years and three weeks since I dragged myself up the stairs to be told by the policemen in my kitchen, one tall one short, that my little sister was dead. Now I've got a Diploma of Grief.

My little sister was forty-two. She had no Grief Diploma but mental illness, hard work, love, she understood.

They say it was a heart attack in her sleep. Comforting, I suppose, better than the suicide I'd always expected. How did she do it? I asked the policeman. That was what I said before I folded up like they do in Hollywood and shouted, No. No. No.

Suicide or heart attack, painfully awake or blithely asleep, she's gone.

What does a Diploma in Grief take?

Weight loss.
Weight gain.
Depression.
Anxiety.
Cuddles from my children, husband, friends.
Better communication with my parents.
Concentrating on work.
Pulling back from my community.
I conduct my Diploma from my bed. It's safe there.

I'm learning, have learnt. I'm more thankful, grateful for the so-called little things: clouds, grasshoppers, love and loving, but I backslide easily.

Tears come whenever they feel like it, a song, a smell, a memory, dreams. I want to hold her hand again. Smaller than mine, hard-worked, warm, her hand fit. I can almost feel it if I remember real hard.

My little sister was always here, on the phone, grabbing a coffee, sometimes in hospital, how is it that now she isn't? How?

All our lives she came up to just past my chin, from my earliest memory of us as kids, bikes, sticky fingers, untidy bedroom, to the last time I saw her, two days before she died, her forehead was mouth height and I'd kiss her brow.

A Grief Diploma doesn't bring back those kisses, the snug of her hand in mine but it can help on the mornings when I have to remind myself she's gone.

I'm learning how to handle sadness. This far along in my grief education: a sudden gust of tears doesn't have to mean a written-off afternoon like it did when I first picked up my pen. Yesterday I was at the supermarket for milk. At the fridge I had a flash of my sister, a hard memory of her not being here and I wanted to lie on the floor and cry. Such a compulsion. I let the thought in, sort of watched it, then it passed.

I couldn't have done that without the Diploma.

Life goes on, people walk their dogs, drive their cars, come and go, and it isn't the insult it was in the early days of her loss. My little sister is part of me, I can access her in the way I do things and the way she said things. Joy can be found in the pain of losing someone, I never knew that. And the word cherish is much more a verb than it could ever have been without my Diploma of Grief.

Wisdom has Come
Roger Vickery

In the multiplex cinema that books my sleep
I might get a week, 10 days at most,
when you are absent from the screen.
But then you return, my phantom star
– to a chair filled room I cannot cross;
on the far side of a quicksand bed;
with or without your lover (usually with);
calling me into a hope-chest maze –
never allowing an air puff
of hope as I twist and turn
in my winding sheets.

They told me – Sherpa counsellors, lantana family,
friends who swim between the flags – once the cut
was made the scar would close like a coffin lid
and under the care of battle-free days,
shrink into a laughter line.

Before I met you for the final time
I encased my Id in Houdini-proof stone.
Afterwards, I thought I could release the boy.
But he's gone to me and daylight.

Wisdom has come and settled.
His winter nest does for my hair.
His uncut nails trail black
as we wait for the show to begin.

After the News

Kathryn Fry

She lies on her bed
hands clenched, her face buried,
legs scissoring the covers.

Her eldest   dead   at twenty-one;
the driver drowsy near Gundagai,
the tree too died at impact.

red eyes raw eyes
       howling
              bury the moon

Someone says the good go young.
Someone gives a cake.
Someone says he's gone to God.

Making porridge for the youngest, she leans
against the stove, her gown undone,
her tears dropping into the mix.

Killed before action in Vietnam,
his Last Post; the coffin lowering,
the soil shifting into her heart.

Orange

Nicole Gill

Orange is the scent of conversation. My brother Richard was never much of a talker.

A shy child, we're not sure when he tipped from social awkwardness to full-blown mental illness. He'd started to slide while I was overseas. Bedridden, my mother said, blood tests showed nothing conclusive. When I flew back, I found him changed.

He could walk again, but he'd acquired a violent paranoia, his world distorted by a monstrous dark upwelling of fear and delusions. We eventually convinced him to check himself into the Psych Ward. He changed his mind about wanting to stay, but we signed the paperwork to keep him there.

Gradually, things improved. Richard moved into his own flat. We all went for dinner for Dad's fiftieth. Wine smoothed over everyone's anxiety - I think we had fun.

A month later, my mother got up to iron some shirts and collapsed by the ironing board. A blood vessel had burst in her brain - she spent the next two years in a coma. We were all watching her, hoping she'd return to us, when we should have been watching him.

Orange is the breath of springtime. One September afternoon, my father rang. Richard hadn't dropped off Nan's groceries. He always dropped them off on a Wednesday.

I drove over to my brother's flat, and knocked on the door. 'Richard? Are you in there? Richard?!' I heard a glass hit the floor.

'RICHARD! Open the door, please!'

Eventually he did and we saw what he'd done.

He'd taken a broken glass, done some experimental scrapes across his pale upper arms, before really getting to work on his wrists. Big gaping trenches, widened with serious intent.

I wrapped his wrists in tea towels, drove him to Emergency. The doctor there snapped questions at him as he daubed his wrists with cocaine for the pain, which, of course, Richard tried to snort as soon as he turned away.

Orange is the smell of hygiene. The next day, we went to clean Richard's flat. We bought an eco-friendly surface cleaner stamped with a cheerful citrus mascot. It cut though the blood, grime, and the kitchen wall paint. My little brother mopped the floor, gagging, repeatedly shooing a neighbourhood cat away from the blood. The scourers, the mop, the orange-scented cleaner - we rammed them all into somebody else's wheelie bin as we left the street.

You didn't die that time, Richard. They patched you up, sent you back to the Psych Ward.

A week later, we take you for a Mother's Day visit to the next floor. Although Mum's still comatose, you wear long sleeves to cover the bandages on your wrists. You cry when we go to visit her. We all do.

They let you out shortly after that. Within a fortnight, you're dead.

Orange is the reek of helplessness, hopelessness, anger, confusion, guilt and despair. You can buy it as air freshener, surface cleaner, washing powder, stain remover, and I cannot escape it.

Orange is everywhere.

Water
Hanna Schenkel

As soon as the water hit her neck she could feel herself relax. She'd reached her third trimester and the water helped her aching back and dry skin. She wished she could make it hotter, so hot her skin would turn bright red. Alas, her doctor had forbidden it.

She willed herself to escape the flood of thoughts that usually carried her through the day: shopping lists, cleaning lists, email lists, finance lists; banished as the water embraced her, reducing her world to warmth.

At first she was confused when she opened her eyes and found the water swirling around her feet had turned a deep, sickening red.

Getting her into her bathrobe was all he'd managed before the ambulance arrived. Droplets of water formed on the tips of her hair like on stalactites, falling intermittently and creating a puddle on the floor of the ambulance. If time stood still, if they would not move again, would little peaks start forming?

He looked strange to her, like a deep sea monster, suspended in his aquarium by tubes, his body squirming with the memory of water. They told her his lungs were not developed enough to sustain life; that her son was struggling to absorb enough oxygen for his brain to function.

Her son. Sun? Wasn't the sun supposed to be warming? She shivered. They'd asked for his name. He looked too small for a name.

The doctor had offered them water but he could not get his arm to lift and pick it up. He was fixated on the glass, waiting for it to move, willing it to move as just moments ago he had done for his son. He could see her reflection in the glass – distorted, pale, a phantom image. She was sitting right next to him but she wasn't there. Where was she?

The silence threatened to crush him, but the doctor had never stopped speaking. It was then he realised death was a sponge, sucking everything into its fabric.

The water was almost scalding her back but she did not move. Her skin was bright red. Wasn't this what she had wanted? Her legs weren't strong enough to carry the guilt. She cowered on the floor, clutching the wilted skin of her vacant belly.

Finally the tears came, joining the hot stream as it got sucked away into the drain.

It didn't look like a coffin. It was too small, more like a chest, a treasure chest, ready to bury his fortune so it could be hidden from the world until he might recover it. He had carved a whale in the lid. He didn't really know why. Maybe because the intended contents had swallowed his wife, taken her captive in their belly and carried her where he could not reach her.

They scattered his ashes in the ocean. The sun set leisurely over the horizon, warming them as they watched their child slowly disappear into the water.

Mum's Place

Kynan Cliff

My wife and I live in separate towns, so, we were eager to see each other, but, in the end, I got drunk on beer and Havana Club and I doubt I was much company at all. We were celebrating her birthday in a country cottage we had rented for the weekend with some friends. I slept late the next day and missed breakfast. In the afternoon, I kissed my wife goodbye and collapsed into the back seat of a friend's car. I tried to ignore the sloshing in my stomach as we lurched along the highway towards Newcastle. When the car finally pulled up at Mum's place, I shoved the door open and stumbled out into a dark and starless world.

I spent that evening with Mum, her partner Chris, and my brother Jacob. Mum cooked lamb and potatoes. She heaped my plate, and Chris' but only took a small portion for herself. Jacob ate his meal on the lounge, watching television. While we ate, Mum hummed and groaned quietly to herself. Nobody said anything.

In the kitchen, I asked Chris what I should do with my leftovers.

'Just put them in the bin,' he whispered, gently lowering his plate into the sink.

The lamb slid off my plate and I covered it with some rubbish. In the past we would have fed our leftovers to our dog, Suzie, but she had died a few weeks earlier. Chris had buried her in the yard and covered her grave with lawn clippings.

I sat out the back with Mum while she smoked cigarettes, her cheeks puffy and wet. We talked about cosmetic surgery. She went on about how terrible celebrities looked with their Botox injections. I kept agreeing with her until eventually she admitted that she had been considering a facelift.

'But then I realised, they don't make you attractive.'

'No,' I said, 'They don't.'

'God, I miss Suzie,' she said.

We talked about other things too. About my brother and how he is in a bad place and lacks confidence. About my Aunt Julie and how sick she is and how Uncle Geoff is too scared to take her to the hospital. The whole time we spoke, Mum peered up into the darkness above the trees. At one point, a rescue helicopter passed over the house, carrying some broken person through the night. Mum crushed her cigarette on the table and went inside to pour herself another wine.

Grief
Lydia C. Lee

The unused coffee cup on the machine might start it.

A bill or flyer addressed to him would make her flinch.

The small dull ache that never seemed to disappear and tears that surfaced unexpectedly when a memory forced its way into her thoughts.

The emptiness. Knowing that nothing can ever change it back. She could never sit close to him again. Or laugh at one of his jokes. Or call him mid-afternoon to see how his day was and what time he'd be home. Little habits that shape a life shared.

Sometimes she even forgot. Waiting to hear the key in the door as the television washed over her.

It was always at night when the painful loneliness resurfaced.

The large, empty bed reminding her that he was gone.

The hardest of all, the intruding thoughts that stole her sleep. The memories of happy times.

The sadness. The futility. The grief.

The hours loomed, offering pain and anxiety. Minutes crawled. Time elastic in the darkness, stretching torturously.

In the morning, she'd be tired but busy with the obligations of the day. The company of others soothingly distracting. Passing the time with activity, but only mildly engaged. A panacea of sorts.

Waiting for something intangible to change. Knowing that it already had.

www.ingramcontent.com/pod-product-compliance
Lightning Source LLC
Chambersburg PA
CBHW050437010526
44118CB00013B/1565